CHATHAM HOUSE PAPERS · 34

INDUSTRIAL

COLLABORATION

WITH JAPAN

D1416962

CHATHAM HOUSE PAPERS · 34

INDUSTRIAL COLLABORATION WITH JAPAN

Louis Turner

with a foreword by Hiroshi Takeuchi

in association with

Ayako Asakura, Reinhard Hild, Michael Hodges,
Ralph-Dieter Mayer, Yoshihisa Miyanaga,
Konomi Tomisawa, Masatoshi Toriihara

The Royal Institute of International Affairs

Routledge & Kegan Paul
London, New York and Andover

First published 1987
by Routledge & Kegan Paul Ltd
11 New Fetter Lane, London EC4P 4EE
29 West 35th Street, New York, NY 10001, USA, and
North Way, Andover, Hants SP10 5BE

Reproduced from copy supplied by
Stephen Austin and Sons Ltd and
printed in Great Britain by
Redwood Burn Ltd, Trowbridge

Library of Congress Cataloging-in-Publication Data

Turner, Louis, 1942-
Industrial collaboration with Japan.

(Chatham House papers ; 34)
"The Royal Institute of International Affairs."
Bibliography: p.
1. Joint ventures – Japan.
2. Joint ventures – United States.
3. Joint ventures – Europe.
I. Title.   II. Series: Chatham House papers ; no. 34.
HD62.47.T87   1986   338.8'8   86-26048

ISBN 0-7102-1109-0

CONTENTS

PREFACE

It is fitting that an international team has carried out this study on industrial collaboration between Japanese and non-Japanese companies and economies. Our team has included Japanese, German, American and British researchers. We have interviewed industrialists and policy-makers in Japan, the United States and Western Europe. We have jointly held seminars in Tokyo, London and Munich.

The geographical distance separating the various researchers has obviously been a barrier, but the fact that Masatoshi Toriihara worked for a year as the MITI visiting fellow at the Royal Institute of International Affairs meant that Japanese views were well represented during the crucial first half of this project. The channels between the RIIA and Tokyo are now firmly established, and in many ways it was the links between London and Munich that still needed further consolidation, partly reflecting the damage that high airfares do to intellectual life within Europe.

Thanks must be given to the following: the Anglo-German Foundation for funding the core of this work at the European end; the National Institute for Research Advancement in Tokyo for covering the Japanese costs; LeHigh University for helping Michael Hodges (the actual initiator of the project) to take part; and MITI, the Long-Term Credit Bank of Japan and the LTCB Research Management Institute for letting some of their staff take part in what has been a non-governmental and non-commercial exercise.

Finally, we must thank all those officials, industrialists and other specialists who contributed their time by being interviewed, attending seminars or commenting on versions of our draft. It would be invidious to single out any by name – too many people have helped us.

Our approach was to ask Japanese and non-Japanese researchers to write in parallel about how industrial collaboration has worked in three key industrial sectors. In the fourth, consumer electronics, I worked without a Japanese opposite number. Three of us also concentrated on how the United States, Japan and Western Europe each saw the issues.

It was decided that I should write this volume, drawing on and summarizing the work of the other researchers, and I have tried throughout to reflect their distinctive views, even when I may not have agreed. Inevitably, there will be parts of this report in which my views come over more strongly than other members would want; for this, I apologize. I, too, take the blame for any errors. The team takes the credit for bringing the project to what I think is a successful conclusion.

October 1986   L.T.

FOREWORD
BY HIROSHI TAKEUCHI

Following the meeting of the Group of Five in the autumn of 1985, the yen sharply appreciated in response to coordinated actions aimed at correcting trade imbalances. Because the yen is likely to stay strong in the longer term, the Japanese government will have to stimulate domestic demand, while private firms will need to accelerate their policy of internationalizing their activities. These corporations have already been stepping up their overseas investment and their industrial collaboration with developed countries, as a way of coping with trade frictions.

In the immediate future, the international division of labour between Japan and its Asian neighbours is bound to increase further, given the remarkable economic and industrial development of the latter. So far, such internationalization has been a one-way action, involving an increase in Japanese exports and foreign investment. However, the appreciation of the yen should encourage imports. At the same time, a growing number of foreign companies are seeking to build Japan into their global investment strategies. It therefore seems that the real internationalization of the Japanese economy is now about to take off.

Given the strength of the Japanese economy, such a development cannot be ignored. However, this internationalization will bring its tensions. For instance, westerners are still often ignorant of Japanese developments, or frightened by the apparent competitive strengths of Japanese companies. They persist in seeing barriers to western participation in the Japanese economy which either are in process of being dismantled or already no longer exist.

These western fears will not be easily soothed. Japanese people tend to be shy in expressing themselves and are relatively inexperienced in international affairs. In some cases, the fact that some Japanese may not perceive that there are other scales and systems of values in the world may create a degree of continued mutual incomprehension.

Our joint study also had to face the problem of such 'perception gaps' at an early stage, as researchers from Japan, the United Kingdom, the United States and West Germany came to work together. However, as the Japanese and western researchers talked to one another and exchanged visits over the course of eighteen months, mutual misperceptions were considerably lessened.

The results of this study are summarized in the following essay written by Mr Turner, who presents an objective analysis of the phenomenon of industrial collaboration between western nations and Japan. He examines the current extent of Japan's internationalization and raises some questions about the relative international inexperience of some Japanese investors. At the same time, he suggests that western companies and governments could do far more to understand the implications of Japan's outward investment boom.

This study is unusual because Mr Turner has based his analysis on specific case studies involving industrial collaboration with Japan. For those western corporations that are searching for the best way to collaborate with Japan, this study will be an excellent guide. It will also be relevant to those Japanese corporations whose concern with internationalization is increasing, in that it will help them understand some common western views on the issues of industrial collaboration with Japan.

Although difficulties remain, international industrial collaboration is an essential strategy for surviving severe international competition. Corporations will find the most effective patterns of collaboration by trial and error. Collaboration, which was previously restricted to the companies of western nations, has now begun to involve Japan as well. In the near future, collaboration between the Newly Industrializing Countries and the developed nations will become equally well established. International industrial collaboration will continue to involve new economies and will further strengthen interdependence within the world economy.

This is the first book for westerners which concentrates on the idea of Japan as a partner for collaboration. I believe that this essay, which is itself the result of a collaborative research effort, will benefit all readers who are concerned with the need for strengthened international collaboration.

1

INTRODUCTION

When Halley's Comet approached the sun earlier this year, it was observed by a number of spacecraft. In Europe, publicity concentrated on the European Space Agency's Giotto space probe, which plunged into the comet's heart, producing dramatic pictures of its nucleus. Less well publicized was the degree to which this European success was the result of cooperation between the space agencies of Western Europe, the Soviet Union, the United States and Japan. In particular, two Japanese spacecraft (Suisei and Sakigake) carried out part of the longer-range monitoring of the comet and contributed to the eventual success of the European mission.

This is a spectacular example of the way in which the Japanese can work in harmony with other countries, and it runs counter to the common stereotype of the Japanese as being 'super-competitors' dedicated to national success at all costs and across all economic sectors. In fact, at a level far removed from space, there are a growing number of cases in which Japanese companies are working with non-Japanese ones to develop products which do not always have an obvious Japanese connection. Among the major products, there are aircraft (Boeing's 767), helicopters (the BK117), aero-engines (the V2500) and automobiles (the Chevrolet Nova, Rover 800 range and the Honda Legend) which have all been produced through some form of collaboration between Japanese and non-Japanese companies. Cases such as these have developed as part of a wider surge in Japanese foreign direct investment, which has recently been given a further boost by the strengthening in the value of the yen to levels which now make exporting from Japan increasingly uneconomic for key industries.

In concentrating on the cases in which Japanese and non-Japanese companies have worked together, this study is focusing on one of the most distinctive aspects of this investment boom: the fact that the Japanese authorities have been officially promoting a policy of 'industrial collaboration' which goes beyond the mere encouragement of Japanese companies to set up factories overseas.

To westerners, the terms 'industrial collaboration' or 'cooperation' seem imprecise (see the beginning of Chapter 2 for a discussion of the issues). However, a fairly representative statement of the official Japanese approach to industrial collaboration can be found in the White Paper on International Trade issued by the Ministry of International Trade and Industry (MITI) in 1982:

> Japan owes its postwar growth to the free trade system. It is the duty of our nation to contribute to the maintenance and expansion of the free world economic order sustained by the tripolar powers – Japan, the US and Europe – doing whatever we can to avoid falling into the pitfall of protectionism. It is necessary from this viewpoint to help solve the structural problems with industry in America and Europe, encourage its revitalization, and form a harmonized international division of labour among them. Japanese industry is keeping up a good performance as compared with its counterparts in the Western nations. Not only should Japanese industry have trade relations with them, but it should also promote mutual exchange in wider areas such as capital, technology and knowhow, and complement and strengthen mutual activity. 'Industrial Collaboration' is a concept that encompasses industrial exchange in a wide spectrum between industrialized nations as described above.

The White Paper then goes on to illustrate typical forms of industrial collaboration, suggesting that it could take the form of mutual investment, technological exchange or collaboration in third markets.

The Europeans and Americans have not always known how to treat such rhetoric. For example, when Toyota wanted to link up with its leading American competitor, General Motors, to create a

Californian joint venture (the NUMMI venture), how were the US authorities supposed to react? Similarly, within Europe, firms like BL (the Rover Group),[1] Volkswagen, ICL (now part of STC), Siemens, Thorn EMI and Thomson are linked in a series of collaborations with such Japanese competitors as Honda, Nissan, Fujitsu and JVC. What are we to make of such deals?

Within Europe and North America, there is considerable scepticism about the motives of the Japanese. In the eyes of many, the latter are seeking to accomplish by disguised investments what protectionist measures are not allowing them to achieve. There is talk of these collaborative ventures being 'Trojan Horses', which will allow the Japanese to establish market dominance without arousing political opposition.

The intensity of this debate can only grow, as the strengthened yen encourages a new wave of outward investment at a time when the Europeans have been moving from a series of initiatives to encourage cross-frontier research collaboration – in sectors such as information technology (the ESPRIT programme) and telecommunications (RACE) – to a more market-oriented pan-European programme covering a wide range of non-military advanced technologies (EUREKA). In all these programmes, the emphasis on encouraging European companies to collaborate with each other could call into question other kinds of collaboration, such as those between European and Japanese companies. If intra-European collaboration is becoming more desirable, does this mean that Euro-Japanese collaboration is thought to be undermining Europe's long-term competitiveness?

These are emotive questions, and the answers will depend upon one's view of what an optimal industrial policy should be. Some readers will be interventionist by nature, believing that the Europeans can learn from Japan's industrial policies in the 1960s and 1970s. In other words, Europe should identify key industries to be nurtured by some combination of preferential treatment within Europe and protection from over-powerful competitors from other continents. Some people, too, will deplore the idea that Japanese investors should be allowed to drive indigenous companies out of business.

Other readers, however, will believe that the best industrial policy is one that maximizes competition, and will thus judge the collaborations by the extent to which they increase the amount of competition

3

in the world economy. Such people will not necessarily be insensitive to demands that competition should be fair as well as free – and some would argue that intensified collaboration within Europe does not have to involve a retreat into Europrotectionism.

In the acknowledgments, the cosmopolitan nature of the research team was mentioned. The fact that its members were willing to work as a team inevitably means that most of them believe that the closer integration of the Japanese and non-Japanese economies is a desirable development. However, this does not mean that the members hold identical views, nor does it mean they all view the collaboration process uncritically.

What I have therefore tried to do in this study is to summarize the work of the team, without trying to leave the impression that its views were unanimous. Given that I am writing for a Japanese as well as a European audience, I have sometimes expressed arguments more delicately than is my usual practice. However, I have not tried to hide the fact that there are arguments – with which I generally disagree – against collaboration with Japan which a Japanese audience may find uncomfortable but would be unwise to ignore. At the same time, there is considerable Japanese impatience with European and North American complaints that the Japanese economy is closed to them – complaints which often come close to implying that Japanese spokesmen are lying. I have worked on the assumption that such disputes need to be brought out into the open.

Finally, since this study was a genuine case of collaborative research, it has certain emphases which stem from the interests of the Japanese members of the team. In particular, they have insisted that it should include the US-Japanese dimension as well as the Euro-Japanese one. Although this has added to its complexity, it has also helped to illuminate the European dilemma. In several parts of the study (particularly those dealing with aircraft), it is clear that the trans-Pacific axis is what really matters to the Japanese. To some extent, relations with Western Europe are an afterthought.

This concept of the Euro-Japanese link being the weakest within the Euro-US-Japanese 'triad'[2] is borne out by investment figures. While the two-way exchange of investment between the European Community and the United States comes to $173.7 bn, and that between Japan and the United States to $23.1 bn, the total for Japan and the EC is a mere $8.5 bn, of which EC investment within Japan is less than $1 bn.[3]

2

WHAT IS INDUSTRIAL COLLABORATION?

One of the earliest discoveries of our research team was that the Japanese and the non-Japanese have different perceptions of what collaboration involves. To the non-Japanese, collaboration means two companies working together, often with joint equity holdings, and with neither company having management control over the other.

The Japanese use the words *sangyo kyoryoku*, which have a much wider meaning than what the westerners understand by collaboration. The Japanese words convey the ideas of common action and collaboration, but also a sense of 'cooperation', whereby economic activities in two countries are linked together. In this latter sense, the Japanese do not just envisage intergovernmental economic agreements, but also 100% foreign-controlled direct investment. Westerners would not tend to count such investment as true collaboration, because it lacks the symmetry of partnership which is inherent in the western sense of the word. On the other hand, the Japanese believe that direct investment involves elements from the two economies working together and thus counts as a form of collaboration.[4]

In particular, the Japanese see collaboration as an integral part of international industrial adjustment. In the words of a recent statement from a high-level study group on Japanese direct foreign investment:

Industrial cooperation through direct foreign investment contributes to increased employment, production and exports, to the vitalization of regional economies, and to the efficient use of resources. It is hoped that a horizontal international division of labor between Japan and other developed countries will develop from industrial cooperation, benefiting both partners. Increased imports into Japan of high quality and differentiated products will help enhance our consumption; those of capital goods, our production ... as one reason behind the present trade friction is loss of industrial vitality and international competitiveness, industrial cooperation through direct investment is an important and urgent task.[5]

In many areas, the Japanese and non-Japanese use the concept of collaboration to cover the same activities. However, the fact that the Japanese define the concept more widely is important, because it may sometimes have led them to believe that the non-Japanese are more enthusiastic about some kinds of industrial activity than is actually the case. There is also concern in the West that the Japanese like to describe as collaboration industrial relationships in which the non-Japanese are in a dependent position, but are less keen to use the term when it comes to ventures in which the non-Japanese dominate.

Types of collaboration
In practice, collaboration is a slippery concept and it is thus worth spelling out the variety of relationships which two companies can adopt when working together – sometimes at levels well below those involving mutual investment. Even if the Japanese do use the term collaboration to cover one extreme – 100% direct investments in which the investing company maintains complete control – there are a number of variants in which no equity investment is involved at all. In fact, there is a spectrum of activities ranging from direct investment, through two companies working together to develop specific projects, to the point at which companies have little more than a bare contractual relationship.

Technical assistance and licensing
At the opposite end of the industrial spectrum to direct investment are such activities as the provision of technical assistance to foreigners and licensing. It is, for instance, possible for one company to sign a technical consultancy agreement with another one that

possesses certain desired technologies. Under such a deal, the latter company will transfer some of its technical know-how in return for a fee. It may well send some of its managers over to the recipient company to ensure that the new technology is utilized effectively.

In the licensing case, a company with some distinctive product will give another company the right to produce it for a fee. However, the danger of licensing is that it strengthens potential competitors. Thus, there will frequently be some restrictions on how the company taking the licence can use it, and licence agreements are often quite specific about which third markets the company taking the licence can export to. Companies providing the technology are often content to receive royalties in return.

The attraction of licensing deals for the recipient company is the access it gains to other technologies without any apparent loss of management control. In some western circles, the use of licensing to sell technology to Japanese companies is now under review, and it is argued that technology has been sold too cheaply to Japan in the past. The result has been a tightening of licensing policy in industries such as microelectronics, with American companies such as Texas Instruments refusing to renew licences for their patents, on the grounds that Japanese competitors have been using cheap American technologies to destroy the American semiconductor industry.[6]

OEM deals

Further along the collaborative spectrum is the OEM – Original Equipment Manufacturing – phenomenon, whereby a company manufactures a product which another company then buys and sells under its own brand name. This is a relatively common practice used by major retail chains, such as Sears Roebuck in the United States or Dixons in the United Kingdom. What is less well known is that manufacturing companies often sell products in their range which have been bought in by this means from competitors.

Normally an OEM arrangement will involve more than just the exchange of signatures on a contract. For one thing, products will often need minor modifications to suit the end market and the companies concerned will negotiate about necessary minor design changes. However, if the producer develops a commercially attractive range of products, it will seek to strengthen its marketing position either by working with, or by finding ways of circumventing, the end-marketer. Inevitably, then, OEM deals are generally seen as temporary affairs, since the stronger producers of OEM goods will seek to attack end-markets either directly or through some other form of collaboration with the end-marketer.

Joint Development

A fairly passive OEM deal will usually evolve imperceptibly into a more active relationship whereby companies work together to develop some part of a new product. This may involve little more than the end-marketer taking the lead on tightening up the technical specifications of the product. However, at the opposite extreme, the design leadership may be almost entirely taken over by the marketing company, with the resultant product being manufactured, in effect, almost under subcontract. There is a half-way position where the end-marketer works actively with leading component suppliers to develop a product which is superior to what could be produced with passively bought-in components.

Equity stakes, joint ventures and consortia

At another point in the spectrum are joint ventures or consortia, in which a number of companies take a stake. Such ventures may well be a way of melding the complementary strengths of the parent companies, but they can also be a convenient way of avoiding direct competition. A more confrontational strategy is that of one company taking a stake in the equity of another – an arrangement which generally tends to be unstable until the stronger partner increases its equity stake to a point at which it establishes effective control.

Westerners do not generally accept acquisitions as a form of collaboration, although technically they come within the Japanese definition of this concept. In practice, such acquisitions are a reasonably common experience in Western Europe and North America, but occur much less often in Japan. Occasionally, when the acquisition occurs because one of the companies has been looking for a 'White Knight' to save it from an unwanted predator, it could be described as 'collaboration', but in general this is not a term that is used of acquisitions.

Joint marketing

There can be agreements between companies to sell jointly in specific markets where, for some reason, neither company feels strong enough to go it alone. One such form of collaboration which the

Japanese often mention is the joint development of third markets – that is, markets in which neither company is particularly well established.

Setting international standards

In recent years, there has been an interesting increase in the number of cases in which companies work together to develop standards for a certain industry. In the course of this study, mention will be made of the kind of work which Philips and Sony carried out to establish a standard for compact disks. There are similar initiatives to create international standards for the eight-millimetre videocamera (camcorder), computer interfaces, and factory and office automation. These attempts are politically complicated, but they have certain aspects in common. In every case, the principal actors know that they have to achieve international support if the proposed standards are to prove effective. However, few Japanese companies are yet involved in such programmes; the collaboration which is taking place is primarily between companies on either side of the Atlantic.[7]

100% foreign-controlled investment

Foreign direct investment in which the investing company has total control can take the form of the acquisition of an existing foreign company, or it can be a 'greenfield' investment, in which the investing company builds its foreign operation up from scratch. One variant, which falls between these two extremes, occurs when the investing company buys unwanted plants from local competitors. This leaves the latter as independent companies, but means that certain activities fall under foreign control.

As already mentioned, Japanese and non-Japanese observers disagree as to whether such investments count as true collaboration or not. But the fact that the non-Japanese do not consider them to be collaborative does not mean that they are hostile to inward foreign direct investment. Nevertheless, they do tend to judge 100% foreign-controlled investments by a rather tougher set of criteria than if they were evaluating a generally accepted form of collaboration, such as joint development programmes or licensing arrangements.

This perception gap is not important in itself, for even a discussion of industrial collaboration defined narrowly on non-Japanese lines will inevitably have to take direct investment into account. The

What is industrial collaboration?

difference of opinion between the Japanese and non-Japanese, therefore, is not over whether direct investment is fundamentally desirable or not, but over whether it is as automatically beneficial to the host economy as the Japanese tend to assume. The debate is about the ways in which the non-Japanese can maximize the returns they receive from Japanese inward direct investment. To many Europeans, it is also about balance, mutual benefits and reciprocity. Given that the Japanese are investing overseas so successfully, surely the non-Japanese should be getting more encouragement to invest in Japan?

3

COLLABORATION AND JAPAN: THE HISTORY

Those with a keen sense of Japan's industrial past will know that its current industrial success was made possible by a policy deliberately aimed at adapting the best of western technology to Japanese needs. In the Meiji era, this policy consisted of a mixture of sending Japanese to study best practice abroad[8] and of commissioning reports from overseas. However, the inflow of technology also came through the direct involvement of non-Japanese companies. Dunlop, one of the world's first great multinationals, established a subsidiary in Japan in 1909, which was later to become Sumitomo Rubber,[9] the company that acquired most of Dunlop's residual European tyre assets in 1984–5. Similarly, NEC was originally a subsidiary of America's Western Electric (now part of General Electric – the US company).[10]

Over the years, other Japanese companies came to work quite closely with foreign companies. A visitor to the head offices of JVC, the company which pioneered the dominant VHS video-recorder system, will be given models of 'Nipper' – the dog which listens to the horn gramophone in the famous old 'His Master's Voice' trademark. This is a relic of the days before World War II, when the company was a subsidiary of RCA. Again, the 'Fuji' in Fujitsu stems from the role that the German electrical engineering giant, Siemens, played in its creation. The German company linked up with the Furukawa Group in 1923 to form Fuji Electric, which in turn gave birth to Fujitsu in 1935. The 'Fu' came from Furukawa, and the 'ji'

11

from Siemens (reflecting the similar pronunciation the Japanese give to 'ji' and 'si').[11]

The postwar period

The onset of World War II inevitably led to a severe reduction in the number of foreign investors in Japan. In the postwar period, the Japanese authorities kept the number of foreign entries to a minimum and only a limited number of non-Japanese companies were able to invest directly. The main penetration was carried out by oil, chemical and metal companies, which were able to invest in Japan during the US occupation. Since 1967, there has been a controlled liberalization of inward foreign investment.

The fact that such investment was actively discouraged for at least twenty years after the war is important, because it meant that Japanese companies wanting access to the best Western technology had to enter into collaborative arrangements with foreign companies. For example, shortly after the end of the war, Matsushita (sometimes better recognized by its Panasonic brand name) formed the Nihon Philips Corporation as a joint venture with the Dutch company Philips, in order to introduce technologically advanced products into Japan. At the time, this venture involved considerable technical transfer to the Japanese partner. Even today, these two companies work closely together.[12]

In key sectors, such as automobiles, inward foreign direct investment was formally banned until the early 1970s, thus enabling Japanese companies to use the licensing strategy to get access to foreign technology. For the Europeans, bemused by the emergence of Japanese competition in the automotive sector, it is ironical that the Japanese auto industry largely rebuilt itself by using European technology. Thus, in the early 1950s, Nissan licensed an Austin model for assembly in Japan and Isuzu struck a similar deal with Rootes. France's Renault licensed one of its models to Hino. At the time, such deals made sense to the Europeans, but 35 years later, with Austin absorbed into the struggling BL and Rootes having been acquired first by Chrysler and then by Peugeot, and both groups facing ferocious competition from the Japanese automotive sector, one can only wonder at how comparative strengths have been turned upside down.[13]

It was only during the 1970s that major foreign multinationals were generally able to start establishing or re-establishing themselves in Japan.[14] Firms like the US auto manufacturers Ford, GM and Chrysler were able to take minority stakes in smaller Japanese competitors, but such investments were still very much the exception. At that time, American companies were looking for ways to get access to the Japanese market, and the only course open to them was to buy into the smaller unprofitable companies.

These smaller Japanese companies were generally unhappy about their enforced links with American giants, and the initial collaboration between the two sides tended to be fairly limited. However, as it became clear during the 1970s and early 1980s that the American industry was lagging behind in such key areas as small car technology, the Japanese partners gained a more influential role, and their American partners are now using them less to get access to the Japanese market, and more to obtain small cars for sale through the established American marketing networks.

The start of outward investment

Until very recently, the Japanese were in a position of technical dependency; they had to enter into a variety of deals with western companies in order to get access to the technology they so badly needed. As the 1950s and 1960s progressed, the technological performance of the major Japanese companies steadily improved, leading first to an export drive and then, more gradually, to an interest in investment. For a number of reasons (including a fear of protectionism), overseas investment picked up steam, often taking the form of collaboration with western competitors.

Initially, however, this investment was directed towards Japan's neighbours, as Japanese companies sought either secure sources of raw materials or a supply of cheap labour. The surge of outward investment triggered speculation that there was something different about Japanese investment: that it was 'trade-oriented' investment, concerned with expanding export opportunities from the economies in which the Japanese invested. It seemed to contrast with the traditional 'trade-destroying' investment strategies followed by the older American and European multinationals.[15]

During the 1970s, the geographical ambitions of leading companies expanded. Firms like Honda, Sony, YKK and Matsushita spread their investments to the United States and Europe. In 1970, for instance, there were only twelve manufacturing operations in the United States in which Japanese firms had more than 50% of the equity. By 1985, there were nearly 400 such companies, and Japan's cumulative investment in American industry made it the third largest investor in the United States after the United Kingdom and the Netherlands.[16] Similarly, just three Japanese investments in the UK during the 1960s increased to fourteen in the 1970s and, by the end of 1985, a further 24 had been established or decided upon.[17]

The motivations of these companies will become clearer later on in this paper. Some of them, such as Sony, deliberately invested abroad, because it was easier to expand overseas than within a highly competitive Japan. Many more, though, started investing in Western Europe and the United States in the late 1970s and early 1980s because rising protectionism made Japan-based exporting strategies increasingly difficult. By 1986, the strengthening of the yen was giving a further boost to outward investment.

Collaboration: a unique approach?

One peculiarity of the growth of outward investment was that it seemed to have the blessing of the Japanese authorities, with the whole operation coming under the guiding concept of 'industrial collaboration'. It was almost as if there was an attempt to reinforce the claimed distinction between the old-fashioned style of investment of past multinational companies, both American and British, and this newer generation of Japanese investors. One Japanese observer has put it this way: 'Japanese firms have a high propensity to "cooperate" because the social and the private benefits of overseas investment are immeasurably high for the Japanese economy ... Japan's multinationalism is definitely taking a unique evolutionary path.'[18]

By the early 1980s, there were enough examples of this kind of collaboration to suggest that its alleged uniqueness might be real. At the corporate level there were a series of ventures in the West in which Japanese and non-Japanese companies were working together. In Europe these included Sony-Wega, GEC-Hitachi, Rank-Toshiba and the J2T case, which involved varying combinations of Japanese, German, French and British companies (not all of these cases were successful). In the United States, this collaboration process culminated in NUMMI, a joint venture in California which was formed to produce a small car and involved a partnership between Japan's largest automotive company, Toyota, and the world's largest such company, General Motors.

It seems that the emphasis on collaboration was seen in some way as contrasting with the competition that conventional forms of direct investment involved. It was further strengthened by the role that governments played in the background in encouraging this kind of collaborative investment. Japanese direct investment was fostered by a series of intergovernmental arrangements, usually – in the case of most European countries – between MITI and its opposite number, but sometimes between a body like the Keidanren (the federation of employers' organizations, which is of considerable importance in Japan) and its opposite number, as was the case in France. The pioneering figure here was Akio Morita, the veteran president of Sony, who had extended his company's activities abroad early in its history. It was he who was to chair the relevant committee of the Keidanren, the Committee on International Industrial Cooperation.

Investment into Japan

Since the early 1980s it has become possible to identify a growing interest on the part of non-Japanese companies in investing in Japan itself. This is a different phenomenon from the type of investment that took place in the Chrysler/Mitsubishi, Ford/Mazda era, when foreign companies were taking advantage of the weakness of Japanese competitors. Companies are now starting to invest in Japan in order to get close to a market which has become a world leader in key areas. For instance, in explaining why his company was setting up a video development centre in Japan, a Philips spokesman stated that, 'Just as Paris is the worldwide centre for fashion and California that for computer chips, so "Japan is the video centre".'[19]

Things have changed. From the days of 'Nipper', when Japanese companies adopted western trademarks and products, we have reached an era in which the world copies the Japanese and, on occasion, creates Japanese-sounding trade names to sell goods bought in from East Asia under OEM deals. One British example is the 'Saisho' brand-name used by Dixons – an apparently meaningless term which sounds very like the Japanese word for 'political fixer'.

15

The growing interest in the strengths of the Japanese economy raises a new set of political issues. Japanese policy-makers point with pride to a whole series of measures designed to open up their economy both to foreign imports and – of more relevance to this study – to investment. They are disappointed when imports and investment do not flood in, and sometimes feel aggrieved when they are criticized for not opening up the Japanese economy sufficiently: they expect foreigners to make a greater effort to take advantage of opportunities available to them.

This issue is important in the wider debate about industrial collaboration. Some non-Japanese argue that the Japanese economy will effectively remain closed, whatever Japanese spokesmen may say. On this assumption, they then argue that the debate about the merits of industrial collaboration is unbalanced, because it concentrates on the extent to which Japanese companies should be allowed to collaborate and otherwise invest in non-Japanese markets, while companies wanting to go into Japan find that they meet much more resistance than apologists for Japan will accept.

Official attitudes

Official Japanese attitudes to both inward and outward investment have varied over the years. In the first two postwar decades, there was a hostile policy towards inward investment and the emphasis was on encouraging Japanese companies to license foreign technology from overseas competitors. This restrictive approach was relaxed in the mid-1960s and the issue now is not whether formal Japanese policy should encourage inward investment, but what the limits to encouragement should be in specific cases.

As far as outward investment is concerned, in the post-1945 era the authorities were more concerned with other matters than with encouraging Japanese companies to invest abroad. However, from the early 1970s the situation gradually changed. Initially some tax measures were introduced which were aimed at facilitating a limited flow of outward investment. After the 1973 oil shock, there was a widely held belief that Japanese outward investment could be used to gain secure access to natural resources – particularly oil and gas. As a result, investments in the oil-producing states were actively encouraged. The view that some energy-intensive, polluting processes should be allowed to migrate to countries close to Japan also gained ground.

This encouragement of resource-related investment had little to do with the concepts of industrial collaboration which started to emerge in about 1980, although there were looser references to 'economic cooperation' before that period, when the Japanese government was already clearly encouraging overseas investment by its companies.[20] However, the momentum did not really start to build up until 1980.

By that time, it was possible to come across statements about the way in which 'Japanese firms are starting to play a key role',[21] and there was an awareness that foreigners were trying to counter Japan's technological dominance by breaking into the Japanese market via joint ventures. However, in the view of Japanese observers, this dominance is even now too narrowly concentrated in a handful of well-publicized industries such as consumer electronics, which leaves the Japanese economy vulnerable in many other important sectors.

As early as 1980, themes emerged in Japanese commentaries which are of particular interest to the non-Japanese. One such theme was the concept that Japanese companies had an 'obligation' to invest overseas in order to bring new Japanese technology to the rescue of western economies which were gradually becoming less competitive. This example again illustrates the perception gap which exists between Japanese and non-Japanese observers. The Japanese on our research team argued that these sentiments are genuinely held, and they pointed to the stream of statements now coming from Japanese opinion-formers and policy-makers about the importance of collaboration as a way of achieving industrial adjustment and a horizontal international division of labour. However, even westerners who are relatively sympathetic to Japanese interests view statements about the obligation to revitalize non-Japanese competition with a certain amount of scepticism. There is quite a common belief in the West that the Japanese are putting forward a series of rationalizations to support a course of action which is being forced upon them by western protectionism and the increased value of the yen.[22] The Japanese, of course, disagree.

By 1981, Japanese concern with industrial collaboration had reached the highest level, following increased protectionist pressures in the US and West European automotive industries.[23] It was a theme emphasized by Prime Minister Suzuki during his visit to Western Europe in June of that year. As well as negotiating on trade

17

issues, such as the spread of so-called 'voluntary export restraints' (VERs), he stressed the desirability of collaboration between Japanese and European companies. He mentioned a number of projects: the J2T venture involving JVC, Thorn EMI and Telefunken; Rolls-Royce's collaboration with Japanese aero-engine companies; Nissan's involvement in Italy and in Spain; and Fokker's potential involvement in Japan's aircraft industry. Some of these projects are discussed later in the paper.

Prime Minister Suzuki also talked of the need for collaboration in third markets, particularly in exporting plant to the Third World. The proposal that collaboration between Japan and the West should be skewed towards joint ventures in parts of the Third World in which Japan is not yet particularly well established is now regularly put forward.

The Japanese government indicated that it was ready to take industrial collaboration further when it tentatively suggested that it was interested in collaborating with the West in advanced high-technology areas, for example in developing VHSIC (Very High Speed Integrated Circuits) and the next generation of computers. There were, however, some Japanese worries about the extent to which Japan's future progress might be held back by its western partners. Even so, these proposals legitimized the idea that governments might work together to develop collaborative research programmes in new areas of high technology. Industrial collaboration finally became official policy in 1982, when it was mentioned in MITI's White Paper on International Trade. Subsequent White Papers have continued to refer to it as a desirable principle for Japan to adopt.

Collaboration and western protectionism

This upsurge in Japanese interest in collaboration with the West was undoubtedly triggered by rising western protectionist sentiments against Japanese goods at a time when protectionism was moving beyond the domain of trade ministers and starting to impinge on foreign policy at the highest level. Throughout the 1970s, protectionist measures against Japanese television exports had been spreading, thus providing the impetus behind the relatively early emergence of the consumer electronics companies as overseas investors. As pressures from American automotive companies grew during 1980–1, trade issues became more sensitive, and VERs were seen to be inevitable if a major political row was to be avoided when Prime Minister Suzuki visited the United States in May 1981.[24]

The VERs agreed in the early 1980s were not enough, however, to defuse political tensions, and it was clear to Japanese officials and executives that investing in end-markets was one way of doing so. But until the value of the yen rose in 1986, there was no strong economic incentive for successful exporters to invest overseas. Toyota, for example, remained highly profitable throughout this period, in spite of the fact that it was the slowest of the major Japanese auto companies to set up plants overseas. Quite simply, exporting made more economic sense than investing.

On the other hand, many Japanese decision-makers did believe that they were doing something more than merely avoiding trade barriers when they invested overseas. The view was widely held that some of the problems associated with collaboration of this kind stemmed from the inadequacies of western economies, and it was felt that Japanese investment could help revitalize them.[25] The 'missionary' element in Japanese investment strategy should not be underrated, even though it may be difficult for most non-Japanese to comprehend or accept as a valid motive.

4

WEST EUROPEAN AND AMERICAN PERCEPTIONS

The pattern of Japanese investment

It is impossible to derive figures for collaborative investment from statistics on Japanese foreign direct investment. Nonetheless, the latter are of interest, because they give an idea of the relative popularity of host countries for Japanese investors. As the statistics in Table 4.1 show, the United States is by a long way the first choice for Japanese investment, playing host to 30% of the cumulative total in spring 1986. Western Europe, as a whole, scores less impressively, with 15.86% of the total, having overtaken resource-rich Indonesia as an investment site only since 1984.

Breaking down the European figures causes some problems, because a variety of measures are used. If all types of foreign direct investment are taken into account, then the United Kingdom is easily the most important host country in Europe, having a cumulative investment of $3,141 million, compared with $1,687m for the Netherlands, $1,343m for West Germany, $1,216m for Luxembourg, $819m for France and lesser amounts for the rest. The reason why the United Kingdom performs so well is that these statistics include investment in services, a sector in which it is particularly strong. At the end of 1983, there were 385 Japanese companies operating in the UK's services sector, compared with 27 in manufacturing and assembly.[26]

Financial services raise some fascinating questions of Anglo-Japanese economic diplomacy,[27] but for the purpose of this study we

Table 4.1 Japan's direct overseas investment by country, cumulative, FY 1951–85

Country	No. of cases	Amount ($m)	% share
North America	13,239	26,965	32.2
USA	12,525	25,290	30.2
Canada	714	1,675	2.0
Central and S. America	4,990	15,636	18.7
Panama	2,374	6,440	7.7
Brazil	1,296	4,587	5.5
Mexico	238	1,330	1.6
Asia	11,530	19,463	23.3
Indonesia	1,381	8,423	10.1
Hong Kong	2,405	2,931	3.5
Singapore	1,775	2,269	2.7
South Korea	1,282	1,683	2.0
Middle East	317	2,972	3.6
Saudi Arabia and Kuwait	4	1,268	1.5
Europe	3,920	11,002	13.2
UK	1,048	3,141	3.8
Netherlands	294	1,687	2.0
W. Germany	758	1,343	1.6
Luxembourg	83	1,216	1.5
France	690	819	1.0
Belgium	242	743	0.9
Spain	148	514	0.6
Eire	58	260	0.3
Italy	138	180	0.2
Other EC	79	136	0.2
Africa	1,110	3,369	4.0
Liberia	637	2,455	2.9
Australasia	1,821	4,242	5.1
Australia	1,209	3,621	4.3
Total	36,927	83,649	100

Source: International Finance Bureau, Japanese Ministry of Finance, Tokyo, May 1986.

are concentrating on the manufacturing sector, where the best-known cases of industrial collaboration have been occurring. Even in manufacturing, the United Kingdom has been in the lead, with Japanese industrial installations employing 12,400 people in 1985, compared with 11,600 in Spain, 10,000 in France and 9,100 in West Germany.[28] But early in 1986, France caught up and moved ahead of the UK in the total number of Japanese industrial plants in operation or planned.

However, when Japan's direct investment flows are put into context, its cumulative overseas investments are still only a third of the United Kingdom's – and the UK is still investing annually two-thirds as much again as Japan was in the early 1980s.[29]

The wider European background

In the 1970s and early 1980s the European countries were concerned more with erecting trade barriers to hold back rising volumes of imports from Japan than with encouraging Japanese investment (whether collaborative or not), which they tended to see as being designed to circumvent trade barriers rather than to revitalize the European economies. At the EC level, relations with Japan since the 1960s have primarily revolved around European complaints about Japanese trading successes, first in clothing and textiles, then steel, followed by consumer electronics and automobiles. These complaints eventually resulted in the 1985 EC-Japan trade understanding, which set quotas for fifteen products from Japan including cathode-ray tubes, colour TV receivers, video tape-recorders (VTRs), fork-lift trucks and numerically controlled machine tools.

Not all discussions between the EC and Japan were entirely negative, for there are some indications that in 1979 the two sides talked about the need to encourage Japanese investment in Europe. In general, though, when the Community did discuss collaboration, it was in the context of the need to redress trade imbalances. Towards the end of 1980, for example, Leslie Fielding, the EC Commission's representative in Tokyo, put all this in a trade context. Once again, issues such as cooperation in third markets were mentioned, but he went one stage further by introducing the concept of a 'horizontal division of labour', in which the Japanese and overseas competitors such as the Europeans would work together in parallel in key parts of the world. On the whole, though, it was left to national initiatives to set the pace. Certainly, by 1980, despite what was happening at the level of trade diplomacy, Japanese observers were becoming firmly convinced that individual EC nations genuinely wanted Japanese investment.

The Federal Republic of Germany

West Germany seemed initially the most logical place in Western Europe for Japanese investment, in that its economy was probably closest in structure to that of Japan. In the mid-1970s, a cluster of Japanese investors established themselves round Düsseldorf. In 1975, Sony acquired Wega, one of the country's best-known producers of audio products,[30] and there were grounds for thinking that Germany might become Japan's favourite investment site in Europe. But it was not to be. It appears that Japanese investors were put off not only by obvious linguistic and cultural barriers, but also by the fact that the Deutschmark has continued to be among the stronger European currencies, thus reducing the Federal Republic's attraction as an investment site. It also seems likely that West Germany's legal requirements concerning worker participation rights[31] may have discouraged those Japanese investors who were already uneasy about dealing with foreign work-forces.[32] Moreover, the federal nature of West Germany worked to its disadvantage, because there was no perceived central effort to attract investment from Japan. Certainly, the Japanese were aware of approaches from the Länder (provinces), such as Bavaria, as early as 1980. However, as these proliferated, the apparent lack of coordination worried them. They tend to respond best to high-level approaches, which in the late 1970s the central government in Bonn was unwilling to make. One of the few intergovernmental deals in the early 1980s was signed in July 1981, and involved an agreement with the Japanese Ministry of Transport to collaborate on the development of a magnetically levitated super-speed railway vehicle.[33]

This is not to say that there was no interest shown by German companies in entering into collaborative arrangements with the Japanese. Volkswagen, for instance, reached an innovative agreement with Nissan, under which the Japanese company builds VW's Santana car under licence, giving VW 1% of the domestic Japanese market.[34] At the same time, Japanese companies such as Hitachi started locating quite sizeable electronics plants in Germany.

German interest in attracting Japanese investment grew in 1981, and the Japanese noted an upsurge in visits from German industrialists. The impression gained was that the Germans now realized the extent to which Japanese companies were starting to move ahead in key electronic and electro-mechanical sectors. Over the next couple of years some important joint ventures were negotiated, such as that between Bosch and Matsushita to produce video-recorders, and the AEG-Telefunken agreement, which was part of the J2T video-recorder venture. Interest also grew in OEM arrangements, with both Nixdorf and Siemens entering into deals in the computing sector.[35]

There is still a degree of ambivalence towards Japan within Germany. Although the two economies have a lot in common in terms of their post-1945 recoveries, the Germans are aware that Japan's success highlights weaknesses in Germany's industrial structure, such as its failure fully to come to terms with the microelectronic revolution. This ambivalence came to the fore in 1986, when Siemens was forced to supplement its collaboration with Philips in the 'Megaproject' with a licence from Toshiba for the latter's one-megabit technology. The licence would probably have caused a political row even if Toshiba had not been a Japanese company, because Siemens was using federal funds to finance the project with Philips, the understanding being that as a result Siemens would be capable of producing its own chips in the one-to-four-megabit range. Nonetheless, the row surrounding this Toshiba licence seemed to have a certain anti-Japanese intensity. This is not totally surprising, since the Philips-Siemens project was intended to produce a European presence in the advanced chip sector which would prove capable of taking on the Japanese competition in the longer run.

The United Kingdom

The success of the United Kingdom in attracting Japanese collaborative investment has been a particularly interesting part of the general European picture. On the one hand, it was perhaps not surprising, since the UK has been the traditional springboard for non-European investors seeking a way into Europe. On the other hand, one would have expected the overvaluation of sterling from the late 1970s to have reduced the country's attractiveness, and likewise its poor reputation in the area of labour relations during the 1970s – a reputation which was particularly worrying for the Japanese, for whom consensus management is a precious goal. The 1974 national miners' strike had, after all, led to the overthrow of Mr Heath's Conservative government, while the 'Winter of Discontent' of 1978–9, during which some parts of the country experienced an accumulation of unburied dead, led to the downfall of the Labour administration then in power.

These factors had not stopped a handful of Japanese companies – notably YKK, Sony and Matsushita – from establishing themselves in the United Kingdom. However, in addition to troubled industrial relations, a streak of anti-Japanese sentiment had emerged in 1977, when Hitachi had sought to locate a television plant in the northeast of England and had run into a storm of protest. This was partly because trade unionists and other television manufacturers had started to feel threatened by Japanese investors, but there were also some objections from local branches of the British Legion (an ex-servicemen's body), whose members still remembered the war against Japan in Asia and the Pacific.[36]

Given this combination of circumstances, which seemed guaranteed to repulse Japanese investment, how did the United Kingdom move into the position during the 1980s of being Japan's preferred investment site in Europe? Obviously, the United Kingdom's linguistic advantages were always likely to swing some investment towards it, but the answer seems to lie in a mixture of industrial policies designed to attract Japanese investors, and in the personal experience of Mrs Thatcher, the incoming Conservative prime minister, whose administration gave the lead on coming to power in 1979. In addition, relatively important British companies entered into collaborations with the Japanese which, with two exceptions, worked well.

It was in the television industry that the United Kingdom's encouragement of Japanese investment started. This industry had in fact had a policy of encouraging Japanese companies to invest in Europe throughout the 1970s. Thanks to the leverage provided by the PAL licence system,[37] it was possible to offer PAL licences in exchange for an acceptance by Japanese companies that they would satisfy European demand from a European – generally British –

base. This explains why firms like Sony and Panasonic started to invest in the UK in the early 1970s.

By the late 1970s, though, this passive acceptance of Japanese investment had turned into a semi-official policy of encouraging Japanese investors in the consumer electronics sector. The full story of this policy development is told later. In outline, a consensus emerged within the sector that Japanese investment should play a specific part in restructuring and reinvigorating the UK CTV industry. This strategy probably represented the first semi-official acceptance that Japanese investment, having been forced into Europe by semi-protectionist pressures, might have a positive role to play. At the very least, it gave the Japanese consumer electronics companies a more positive status in the UK than was being accorded to them elsewhere in Europe.

In addition, Mrs Thatcher came into power in 1979 with a particularly favourable (although probably mistaken) view of the Japanese economic environment. Her views were formed during a visit in 1977 to Tokyo as leader of the opposition.[38] While there, she apparently came to the conclusion that the Japanese economy was a model of free enterprise. Once in power, she immediately began encouraging Japanese companies to invest in the United Kingdom. Initially, this encouragement took the form of exhortations to individual industrialists, an approach which was also followed by Kenneth Baker, the Minister of State for Information Technology during the years 1981–4. In 1981, these isolated unsystematic cases of encouragement were supplemented by the first intergovernmental agreement between Japan and a European country which had the specific aim of encouraging industrial collaboration.[39]

At the corporate level, too, UK companies chose to respond most enthusiastically to the chance of collaborating with their Japanese opposite numbers. Rolls-Royce, Thorn EMI, ICL and the Austin-Rover Group all entered into collaborations which have worked reasonably smoothly (see later sections for details). However, the culmination of British encouragement of Japanese involvement came with the drive to persuade Nissan to invest in the UK. Although it is clearly not what is normally understood by 'collaboration' in Western Europe, the Nissan project has taken on a symbolic role in economic relations between the two countries. Negotiations have proved difficult on such issues as the proportion of local content which the project should purchase from Britain and Europe, but, at the time of writing, the expansion of the project is being accelerated by Nissan, because of the rapidly strengthening yen.

France

For a number of decades, France has run inconsistent and inconstant policies in relation to inward foreign direct investment – be it American, Japanese or, even, European. During the early 1980s, French policies towards Japanese investment were less consistently welcoming than those of the British, though the French authorities are now courting the Japanese with great enthusiasm and France currently leads Europe in terms of the number of Japanese manufacturing investments. In fact, the French government was the first European one to suggest some form of intergovernmental collaboration when, in 1980, it proposed joint efforts in seven industries, with specific reference to collaboration in third markets. In the words of a Japanese journalist, this was 'the first instance of an EC nation making a specific proposal to Japan'.[40]

In 1981, however, when President Mitterrand came to power at the head of a socialist administration, Franco-Japanese relations deteriorated. There was a swing towards a more nationalistic policy which tended to treat Japanese investors with some suspicion. One potential collaboration between Thomson and JVC was actually rejected by the government, while the notorious 'Poitiers incident', in which all video-recorders had to be routed through Poitiers, was essentially a protectionist act targeted at the Japanese.

During 1983–4, French policy softened. The Thomson-JVC collaboration went ahead after some subtle manoeuvres by the Thomson management.[41] Then, in 1983, Dunlop France was forced to file for bankruptcy in the aftermath of the purchase by Sumitomo Rubber Industries of Dunlop's British and German tyre-making facilities. With some 7,000 jobs at stake, the French government was forced to induce Sumitomo to take on the French operation as well.[42] Since then, French policies have been positive towards Japanese investment, and it is clear that the Japanese business community is responding – though some argue that it is in fact still responding to the relative protectionism of French trade policy.

27

Other European countries

Two of the earliest bidders for Japanese investment were the Republic of Ireland and Belgium – two countries with a history of hard marketing and providing lavish incentives in order to attract any form of foreign investment, Japanese or otherwise. Ireland had an early success when it attracted an investment from NEC in 1974. Later on, in 1980, it started to interest Fujitsu, which noted the involvement there of Amdahl, the American computer company, in which Fujitsu has a stake. Belgium was less successful in attracting spectacular Japanese investments, but it had the reputation of being reasonably enthusiastic in its efforts to do so.[43]

Of the major EC economies, Italy has the worst record in attracting Japanese investments, with only eight manufacturing ones up to the end of 1984. Language difficulties and the country's notorious labour relations probably explain this disappointing record. A collaboration between Nissan and Alfa-Romeo has by all accounts been a not entirely happy experience.

Spain, which only recently joined the EC, ran neck and neck with Germany as first choice investment site for Japanese manufacturers for much of the 1970s. Japan's enthusiasm has declined somewhat since then, but Spain still remains an important location for its investment.

European approaches summarized

It was inevitable that the European nations would view the rise of competition from Japan with some suspicion, given the thoroughness with which Japanese companies were penetrating the markets established by West European companies. It was also inevitable that initial European reactions would be negative, given that the emergence of Japanese competition in its full force coincided with the adverse effects on the world economy of the post-1973 oil-price shocks.

Slowly, European governments withdrew some of their reservations about the role that Japanese investment could play in reinvigorating European industry. There were, however, some years of very acrimonious argument within the EC about whether there should be free circulation of goods originating from third countries – an issue which got increasingly complicated as Japanese investors began operating European plants which used quite high proportions of components and sub-assemblies from Japan. Ground rules have emerged and individual European nations are starting to compete fairly strongly for incoming investment. Italy and (on occasion) France have been particularly wary of the implications of European dependence on Japanese investment, but both (Italy less so) have gradually joined the rest of Europe in the competition to attract the next investment to be made by one of Japan's leading companies.

The attitude towards Japanese investment and collaboration has been complicated in recent years by an upsurge of interest in intra-European collaboration through programmes like ESPRIT and EUREKA. To some extent, programmes such as these present Japan as Europe's main competitor. However, even as collaboration within Europe has been increasing, the welcome to Japanese investors has stayed reasonably constant.

Throughout this period, there have been few *causes célèbres* in labour relations with Japanese companies. In the United Kingdom, since the initial storm over Hitachi's proposed television plant in 1977 subsided, trade union reaction to inward Japanese investors has been fairly muted. It is not as though the Japanese have been traditional in their approach to labour relations, for they have stressed single-union deals and no-strike agreements. However, they have recognized that, in the European context, union recognition of some sort is probably necessary. What they have done (skilfully) is to get radical commitments from the traditional European trade unions. Of course, Japanese investors do benefit (as have previous inward investors) from the fragmented nature of the European trade union movement. For instance, there was a nasty dispute between the local French unions and Sumitomo Rubber when the latter acquired Dunlop. However, because of the weak links betweennational trade union movements in Europe, this dispute had little impact outside France.

The United States[44]

The prime destination?

European readers need to appreciate that the Japanese see Western Europe as a side-show compared with the USA. The United States is the single most important location for Japan's overseas investment, accounting for over a quarter of the total. As with

Europe, this investment is a relatively recent phenomenon. In 1973, Japan's direct investment in the United States was a mere 0.7% of total foreign investment there. By 1983, Japan had moved into third place (after the United Kingdom and the Netherlands) with 8.2% of the total. It should be noted, though, that the majority of this investment was in the wholesale trade ($7.6 billion) compared with only $1.7 bn in the manufacturing sector. Indeed, in manufacturing, Japan comes only seventh as an investor in the United States, with the Netherlands, the United Kingdom, France, Germany, Switzerland, Canada and the Netherlands Antilles well ahead.

The automotive sector contains a particularly rich crop of collaborative cases. All three of the American auto giants have equity links with Japanese companies: Ford with Mazda; Chrysler with Mitsubishi; and GM with Isuzu, and more recently with Toyota. The tie-up between GM and Toyota has been spectacular, involving as it does the Californian joint venture known as NUMMI. There are also direct investments (either on-stream or planned) by Nissan, Honda, Mazda, Toyota and Subaru.

In other sectors, there is the well-known case of Fujitsu's equity stake in Amdahl. Hitachi and National Semiconductor are linked through a jointly owned plant manufacturing semiconductors in the United States. There have also been some significant acquisitions, such as Alumax's takeover of Howmet Aluminum; and Nippon Kokan KK has a 50% stake in National Steel. The largest US supplier of industrial robots is GMF, a joint venture between GM and Fanuc, the Japanese market leader.

American reactions

By the end of 1984 there were 370 recorded Japanese manufacturing investments in the United States. The American response has been as ambivalent as the European one. The federal government has played a limited role in encouraging Japanese investment, with the US Department of Commerce and the Embassy in Tokyo running 'Invest in the USA' seminars. In general, however, much has been left to individual states, some of which, like Tennessee and Illinois, have been quite keen to attract it, and in early 1986 more than twenty state governments had offices in Tokyo to encourage inward investment.[45] Others, for example Colorado, have been less enthusiastic. Its governor, Richard Lamm, was quite specific: 'I do not want the Japanese coming in and buying up American technology. I do not want them in our state. I don't want the Arabs owning our banks or the Japanese owning our means of production.'[46]

The states may be taking the leadership in going out to encourage inward Japanese investment, but it is the federal authorities which have the power to block developments through the enforcement, for instance, of US anti-trust law. In the late 1970s, the assumption was that Japanese ventures with American companies tended to be anticompetitive. Thus the Justice Department decided to veto a Hitachi-GE colour TV deal (which had nothing to do with the Hitachi-GEC venture in the UK – confusingly, GE and GEC are separate companies, American and British respectively). This was despite the fact that GE was only sixth in the US market, while Hitachi was twelfth without, at that time, a US manufacturing base.

By the early 1980s, hostility to Japanese imports had increased, but there was a growing interest among the states in competing for the investment which was generated by protectionist pressures. At the same time, attitudes in Washington became more positive towards the contributions which inward Japanese investment could make. The test case came with the NUMMI joint venture, which teamed GM, the leading auto manufacturer in the United States, with Toyota, its Japanese opposite number. If the criteria used to block the 1977 GE-Hitachi deal had again been applied, there would have been no hope for the NUMMI venture. GM, however, made the case that it needed such a venture to gain from Toyota's proven record in developing successful small cars. Despite considerable opposition from GM's other competitors, the NUMMI deal was approved by the Justice Department. Chrysler's response was to bow to the apparent logic of this approval by strengthening its equity holding in Mitsubishi, and by entering into a joint venture of its own (Diamond Star Motors) to produce cars in Normal, Illinois.

On balance, the Japanese are happy investing in the United States, which is seen as the world's richest, most genuinely free market. The degree of competition between the individual states means that there are always some suitors at the local level who are keen to entice Japanese investment to their part of the country.

Compared with the West European experience, the US one has some distinctive features. First, no collaborative deal in Europe has

31

had quite the symbolic importance of NUMMI, bringing together as it does the largest Japanese and non-Japanese automobile companies. Second, owing to the overvaluation of the dollar during 1984 and 1985, the strength of anti-Japanese feeling on trade matters grew to an intensity which has not been fully matched in Europe. Third, the American trade union movement, which originally welcomed Japanese direct investment, has recently taken a more negative position than its more fragmented European counterparts – though, since the US movement is relatively weak by European standards, that may not have mattered too much.

Japanese companies are perceived in the United States as being anti-union (particularly by the UAW, which has had to struggle to get recognition in the auto sector). Neither the Nissan plant in Tennessee nor the Honda one in Ohio are unionized. In the case of the NUMMI venture, which involved Toyota taking over the management of an existing, run-down GM plant at Fremont, the Japanese management forced the UAW to relax its job-classification requirements and to accept a hiring policy which drew only partially on the existing work-force.[47] In another case, Mazda, which recognizes the UAW in its Michigan plant, refused to take over from Ford until the UAW accepted a $7.50 reduction in the hourly wage-rates which Ford had been offering. This differential is supposed to be closed eventually, though it is not clear how quickly.

Labour disputes involving Japanese plants in the United States are still rare. In October 1985, there was a 21-day strike at Sanyo's Arkansas television and microwave factory – the second since Sanyo took the plant over from an American company in 1977. Reports of this strike suggest that, despite the mystique which has built up around Japanese management, Sanyo, at least, had not been able to change the work attitudes of its labour-force as much as it would have liked.[48] No doubt other Japanese companies taking over existing plants and work-forces could also face problems but, generally, the Japanese are being careful to erect greenfield plants where possible, or at the very least to insist on restructuring the labour-force if they are compelled to take one over.

Finally, American concern with national security has had an impact on Japanese investors in a way which has had no precise parallel in Europe. For instance, Kyocera was forced to reverse its 1983 acquisition of Dexcel Inc., a manufacturer of devices used in the avionics of F-15 and F-16 fighter aircraft, and Nippon Steel was prevented from acquiring Special Metals, an Allegheny Corporation subsidiary which produces superalloys used in airframes and engines. In both cases, the Japanese consider that the Department of Defense was a decisive influence behind the scenes.

5

THE CONSUMER ELECTRONICS SECTOR

We now turn to a more systematic analysis of industrial collaboration in four sectors: consumer electronics, information technology, automobiles and aerospace. We adopted a sectoral approach, since it allowed the Japanese and non-Japanese researchers on the project to debate their various perceptions of developments in key industries. It also allowed the team to concentrate on industries with very different underlying competitive positions. Thus, consumer electronics is a sector in which the Japanese are now moving well ahead of their non-Japanese competitors. In contrast, the aerospace sector is one in which the non-Japanese have a long technological lead which they are not likely to have to surrender. Somewhere in the middle are the automotive and information-technology sectors. The Japanese believe that their industrial success is narrowly based, and that non-Japanese observers are assuming too much when they claim that the Japanese will inevitably repeat in other industries their past successes in shipbuilding, steel and consumer electronics.

In this context, our analysis of the aerospace industry was particularly rewarding, because its conclusions run counter to much conventional wisdom. Moreover, we could probably have strengthened this unfashionable point of view by picking other areas, such as chemicals or certain financial services, in which Japan's competitive weaknesses are more apparent than its strengths.

Why study consumer electronics?

Consumer electronics is a messy sector. It covers a range of products, including colour televisions (CTVs), video-recorders (VCRs), black-and-white televisions, radios, hi-fi systems, cordless telephones and cellular telecommunications generally, domestic appliances and home computers. The future holds out the prospect of a further range of products which are of potential interest to consumers: compact disc players, camera cassette recorders, videodiscs, home security systems, etc. Increasingly, the various items produced in this sector are being grouped under the general concept of 'home electronics', the assumption being that they will increasingly interact with each other in the home.

An analysis of the consumer electronics sector is of significance to a study of industrial collaboration for a number of reasons. First, it was Japanese consumer electronics companies such as Sony and Matsushita which, in the early 1970s, helped to pioneer the Japanese investment boom in Western Europe and the United States. Second, the consumer electronics sector is an important mass market for electronic components in a period when the ability to stay at the forefront of microelectronics is usually a significant indicator of general industrial competitiveness. This is not necessarily the case in the United States, where high defence spending provides a cushion for the whole electronics sector. However, it is true of Japan, where consumer electronics provides the industrial stimulus, and – to a lesser extent – of Europe. Third, in contrast with defence spending, the mass markets of the consumer electronics sector provide the stimulus which helps to pioneer the application of automated manufacturing techniques within the electronics sector as a whole. There is thus a major qualitative difference between the impact that the defence industry has on the electronic infrastructure and that produced by consumer electronics.

The final reason for looking at consumer electronics is that this is the sector in which the Japanese most clearly lead the world. The Europeans and Americans have little cause for optimism. Only Philips is in the same category at the global level as Matsushita, Sony, Toshiba, Hitachi, Sanyo and JVC. American companies, such as RCA and Zenith, have lost their ability to innovate, although ITT still has some strengths. In Europe, companies such as

Thomson and Thorn EMI are no longer really at the cutting edge of consumer electronics, though the French company remains ambitious.

Japanese consumer electronics

Today's world-beating Japanese companies were not always so strong. Nearly all of them went through a period in the 1950s when they were heavily dependent on technology and products from foreign companies. Matsushita is a case in point. In the period immediately after 1945, it entered into two joint ventures with Philips – one in Japan and one in Belgium. Any European contemplating the list of products with which Philips helped Matsushita can only smile wryly in retrospect. It included lamps, transistors, and vacuum and TV tubes – all currently basic commodities in the electrical industry. It can be argued that at least Philips had the global vision even then to be concerned with Japan. On the other hand, due credit must be given to Matsushita and its Japanese competitors for having used foreign technological assistance to turn themselves into world leaders in their own right. The current question for non-Japanese readers is whether western companies can reverse the technological flow through strategic alliances with dominant Japanese companies.

The fact that the Japanese have overtaken the international competition in consumer electronics in so short a time is even more remarkable given that a large segment of the European industry was protected during the 1960s and 1970s by the PAL and SECAM patents, which, between them, covered the television systems in use in Western Europe. The PAL licence, which covered the system to be found in most European countries, was deliberately used to encourage Japanese companies to invest in (rather than export into) Europe. This conditional access to PAL technology was one of the main reasons behind the early CTV investments which Sony and Matsushita made in the United Kingdom in 1974 and 1976 respectively.

By the end of the 1970s, Japanese consumer electronics companies had moved to the forefront of the world industry. This was not a development which was masterminded by MITI. Firms like Sony and Matsushita were relatively small at the end of the Second World

War and were sometimes hindered by MITI officials, as was the case, for example, in the 1950s when Sony set about acquiring transistor technology. Most of what has happened since the 1950s can be put down to successful entrepreneurship. Japanese companies were simply more adept than the foreign competition at seeing how microelectronics could be applied to consumer electronics products. MITI certainly channelled its efforts into the general area of electronics, but consumer electronics companies were not the main beneficiaries.

During the 1960s, Japanese companies managed to reduce their costs substantially through a combination of offshore processing and steadily improving economies of scale. This enabled them to achieve a degree of export penetration into western markets, and lured the American industry into the fallacious assumption that cheap labour was all that lay behind the Japanese success. In the early 1970s, the Japanese increased their application of electronics to TV manufacture, which led both to a reduction in the number of components per set and to a higher level of automation in TV assembly. They were compelled to make some overseas investments in order to get round trade barriers, such as the PAL licence in Western Europe, and to avoid being implicated in the growing number of legal and political attacks on imports in the United States.[49] In general, though, they persisted with their export strategy.

By the late 1970s, the Japanese were strong enough to innovate in their own right. The video-recorder is an example of this. Although there was VCR technology in professional recording studios, Philips was initially the only serious competitor for the Japanese in the race to miniaturize this technology and thus produce what was, effectively, a new product. The VCR is now the leading consumer electronics product in world trade, and Japanese companies have been responsible for over 90% of world output. All the indications are that they will maintain their world lead through a combination of high spending on new product research, meticulous attention toproduction technology, further improvements in their design skills (which are already high) and the continued strengthening of their international marketing and distribution systems.

The United States
The Japanese at first met remarkably little resistance from

established US companies, because the latter mistakenly believed that the new challenge was based on cheap labour. Accordingly, such American firms as GE, RCA and Zenith moved operations to East Asia and Mexico, thinking that this would reduce their production costs. In the meantime, the Japanese were revolutionizing the production economics of the industry by applying microelectronics to what had become mature products. Once it became clear that imports from Japan were not being stemmed, US industry resorted to legal proceedings which culminated in 1977 in an orderly marketing agreement.

Japanese companies had seen the writing on the wall and had started investing in the United States. Sony had already built a plant in San Diego in 1972. Matsushita and Sanyo bought out American-owned TV plants in 1976, and Mitsubishi, Toshiba, Sharp and Hitachi all launched US factories. By the mid-1980s, RCA, GE and Zenith had become classic 'hollow corporations' in this sector – that is, 'manufacturers that do little or no manufacturing ... (which) perform a host of profit-making functions – from design to distribution – but lack their own production base.'[50] In particular, they lost the ability to innovate successfully. RCA's attempt, which was a failure, to develop its own videodisc format represented the only recent American effort of any significance to develop a product independently of the Japanese.

The US industry has had to turn to Japanese companies for products under OEM deals. This has led to a situation in which, for example, RCA has some 20% of the American VCR market, but the products are actually made in a Hitachi factory (and before that, they came from Matsushita). Similar agreements with other companies helped to disguise the fact that until the second half of 1986, not a single video-recorder – the leading consumer electronics product of the decade – was being made in the United States. The same situation still holds true for audio compact disc players.

The paradoxical outcome of such developments is that the only company seriously trying to tackle Japanese competition head-on in the United States is the American subsidiary of Philips, the Dutch electronics company. Its top executives point to the knock-on effects of the American industry's capitulation. The resultant collapse of a components industry dedicated to consumer electronics means that the United States is no longer a logical place in which to locate the production of a mechanically demanding product like the VCR.

Yet, if the United States fails to develop VCR production, then, in the words of Mr Wisse Dekker, until recently the president of Philips, it opts out of 'the technology which goes with the VCR: lasers, ceramics, heads, magnetics and a thousand other things ... If you drop out of the learning curve, you will never get back in.'[51]

The US consumer electronics sector is an interesting case in that, after the initial burst of protectionist pressure in the mid-1970s, US companies effectively withdrew from direct competition with the Japanese. There are a handful of genuine collaborative deals, such as the one between Toshiba and Westinghouse to produce CTVs; in general, though, Japanese companies have invested enough to counter the protectionist moves on CTVs, but they have not really deepened their investments. They have tended to move on to products which are at the cutting edge of consumer electronics, such as microwave ovens and compact discs.

Europe

The picture in the United States contrasts with that in Europe, where companies and governments have fought hard to keep some indigenous capacity in this sector (see Table 5.1). The final result may not be much more encouraging than in the United States, but, because the Europeans have been working more deliberately with the Japanese, they have managed to hold on to more of the underlying infrastructure than the Americans have. This could turn out to be an advantage for Europe once the distinction between consumer electronics and professional systems which integrate computers and telecommunications becomes blurred.

Sony and Matsushita were encouraged to invest in the United Kingdom in the early 1970s. Then a turning point came in 1977, when Hitachi sought to establish a greenfield TV plant in the northeast of England. This initiative attracted a great deal of hostility. UK competitors claimed that the plant would add extra capacity to an industry already plagued with overcapacity, and pressure was therefore put on Hitachi to find an established British partner. As a result, it formed a joint venture with GEC to share in the running of one of the latter's existing television factories in Hirwaun, Wales. Similarly, Toshiba formed a joint venture with

Table 5.1 Industrial collaboration in consumer electronics involving Japanese companies in Europe

---

*Direct investment**
Aiwa (UK), Akai (France), Hitachi (UK), Hitachi (W. Germany), Hitachi-Maxell (UK), JVC (W. Germany), Matsushita (UK), Matsushita (Spain), Mitsubishi (UK), Pioneer (Belgium), Sanyo (UK), Sanyo (Spain), Sony (UK), Sony (W. Germany), Sony (France), Toshiba (UK), Toshiba (W. Germany).

Joint venture
J2T (France, UK, W. Germany), GEC-Hitachi (UK),† Rank-Toshiba (UK),† Blaupunkt-Matsushita (W. Germany).

Technology transfer
Philips-Matsushita (Netherlands), Thomson-JVC (France).

---

* Compare direct investment in the USA: Hitachi, Matsushita, Mitsubishi, Sanyo, Sharp, Sony, Toshiba.
† Dissolved.

Rank to run a factory in Plymouth. Sanyo wanted to make a direct investment, but it was only able to do so by acquiring an unwanted television factory in Lowestoft from Philips. Mitsubishi made a similar move and acquired a redundant Scottish plant from Tandberg.

By the late 1970s, UK policy towards Japanese companies had undergone a dramatic change. The British industry formulated a fairly specific policy, working through the relevant Sector Working Party of the National Economic Development Office (NEDO).[52] The Boston Consulting Group was hired to carry out a study on the comparative performance of the British and Japanese CTV industries. Its seminal report emphasized the point that Japan's success was no longer to any significant extent based on cheap labour, but resulted from the vast quality and production-cost gaps which had emerged between Japanese and British products. The NEDO group devised a strategy for the British-based industry, which encouraged it to restructure round three poles: the British company Thorn EMI, its Dutch competitor Philips, and the Japanese companies which were prepared to use existing plant. This seems to have been the first time that any official or semi-official body in the non-Japanese OECD world specifically drew up a strategy in which inward Japanese investment was an integral part.[53]

Elsewhere in Europe, policy towards the Japanese competition took two forms. In France and Italy, there were long-standing unilateral restrictions against Japanese imports. The French chose not to encourage Japanese investors, deciding instead to build up Thomson as a national champion. The Germans, on the other hand, seemed more relaxed about Japanese imports and investment, though they became worried about trade issues in the early 1980s, and supported European Community measures against Japanese imports in 1981.[54]

West Germany's approach produced mixed results. Established companies, such as Grundig and Telefunken, faltered under increasing global competition, and these two companies fell under Dutch and French influence respectively. The federal authorities played a relatively passive role in these developments, accepting the general EC drift towards protectionism in this sector, but distancing themselves from the French position. At the same time, because of its buoyant market and strong tradition of precision engineering, West Germany remained an attractive investment site for Japanese consumer electronics companies. This engineering tradition has been a particularly important consideration for the Japanese, because considerably more electro-mechanical components are used in video-recorders than in conventional television production.

France's position has been particularly complex. It has been strongly committed to establishing its national champion, Thomson, as a credible international competitor – and indeed encouraged it to move into Germany – and it has maintained its protectionism against imported TV sets, tubes and video-recorders from Japan. This negative approach to Japanese goods even spilled over into a short-lived attempt to block Thomson's arrangements with JVC, the Japanese video-recorder company. However, France is currently giving a much warmer welcome to Japanese investment and is picking up some of the investment in this sector which would normally have gone to the United Kingdom and Germany.

Failed collaborations in the United Kingdom

There has been some debate over what constitutes a successful or a failed industrial collaboration. Two collaborations in the United Kingdom – between GEC and Hitachi, and Rank and Toshiba – fell apart and would seem, therefore, to have failed. However, the end results were actually more positive.

These two ventures were conceived at a time when the UK industry was still fragmented, suffering from over-capacity and hostile to the idea of Japanese companies creating new capacity through inward ivestment. Both Hitachi and Toshiba responded by finding joint-venture partners which, inevitably, were among the weaker elements of the industry. The problem with these ventures was that the UK partners had little to contribute in terms of production expertise, marketing strengths and the development of new products. There was little sign that the UK managements thought they could learn anything from the Japanese. In the GEC-Hitachi case, television sets produced on the same production line for the two partners to sell under their respective brand names could be sold at a premium by the Japanese, because Japanese sets already had a higher reputation for quality. It has been argued that the level of UK management assigned to both these projects was too low to earn the respect of the Japanese and that, in any case, there was not enough continuity of personnel on the UK side. In one case, senior Japanese managers were offended when they were greeted by a very senior British executive with his feet on his desk.

In the circumstances, the failure of these two ventures was hardly surprising. In effect, the Japanese were the stronger partners in nearly every area, probably even industrial relations. The joint ventures were supposed to introduce the Japanese to the British way of handling labour relations, but in commenting on the collapse of the GEC-Hitachi venture, Hitachi's president, Mr Katsushige Mita, suggested that 'there was not enough communication between management and labour'. British accounts confirm his view.[55]

In both cases, once the joint ventures were dissolved, the Japanese restructured work practices in the plants which they inherited. Toshiba pioneered one of the earliest deals in which the Electricians' Union (the EEPTU) negotiated a no-strike arrangement and became the sole representative of the labour force. Mr Mita noted that the various unions in the Hitachi plant had appointed a common representative to negotiate with the new Japanese management and commented: 'Things appear to be going much more smoothly now.'[56]

From the point of view of the UK partners, these two joint ventures were unqualified failures. However, as far as the wider UK economy was concerned, the outcome was not very serious. The Japanese companies ended up with existing TV assembly capacity. Neither Rank nor GEC were viewed as part of the industrial core around which long-term restructuring might take place. It did not, therefore, matter if they withdrew from the CTV sector. Few people blame the Japanese for what happened, and they seem to have managed the plants well since then. There is some doubt about whether the plants are actually profitable – it has been reported that the Hitachi one is not[57] – but any lack of profitability has more to do with the Japanese companies' limited market share than with inefficiencies in running the plants. In sum, these ventures were irrelevant collaborations which were forced on the Japanese by UK industrial opinion. Given that UK policy was to limit the disruption caused by the incursion of investors from Japan, they had their positive side.

The J2T video-recorder collaboration

The J2T venture contrasts with the short-lived GEC-Hitachi and Rank-Toshiba collaborations. It involves a larger cast of players: JVC on the Japanese side; Thorn EMI in the United Kingdom; France's Thomson; and Telefunken, Thomson's German subsidiary. It has factories in more than one country: Germany and Britain. In some areas of this complex European and Japanese venture there are signs that collaboration has been increasing.

The venture came about as a result of JVC developing the VHS format video-recorder. This was a technically complex product by the standards of television manufacturing, and very much one which had to create its own market. JVC was a moderately large company with limited overseas operations. In order to make the product successful, it needed to establish it against incompatible VCR formats from Philips and Sony. Although it was a 51% owned Matsushita subsidiary, JVC could not apparently count on immediate support from the parent company, the main reason being that Matsushita had developed a competing product (though its top management soon adopted the VHS format as standard).

There was still enough technical development work to be done on the product to keep the JVC management fully stretched, so it decided to find partners in Europe to help develop new markets. Because the colour television market had become relatively mature,

European manufacturers were delighted to have a new product they could sell on an OEM basis. But the real breakthrough for JVC came when Thorn EMI decided to opt for the VHS format. Thorn is the market leader in television rental chains in the United Kingdom, and it used its highly developed network to persuade consumers to experiment with what was then a relatively expensive and technically uncertain product.

The domination of the UK market by the rental chains meant that, for a short time at least, the United Kingdom probably had the highest per capita penetration of VCRs in the industrialized world. Even today, it is second only to Japan. JVC managers acknowledge that it was this deal with Thorn which determined that the VHS format would come to dominate Europe, brushing aside the competing Philips and Sony formats. This success in Europe also influenced developments in the United States.

Other European companies marketed JVC's VCR, and pressures grew for some form of local assembly. JVC did not apparently consider a greenfield investment; instead, it negotiated with a number of European companies about creating a joint venture and finally chose Thorn EMI in the United Kingdom, Thomson in France and Telefunken in West Germany – all of which had some existing production expertise. The form of the venture was influenced by considerations of scale, because Europe could not simultaneously support optimum-scale plants in Germany, France and the United Kingdom.

In cooperation with JVC, Thorn and Telefunken formed a venture, known as J2T, to operate a video-recorder plant in Berlin. In May 1981, the French company Thomson-Brandt joined the group, and the venture was called J3T. The agreement was that the four partners would have equal equity stakes in the venture, and would manage three factories: one making video-recorders in Germany, one making videodisc equipment in the United Kingdom, and one in France manufacturing the cameras needed for these products.[58]

The venture soon underwent further change. In 1981 Thomson was nationalized and was forced to pull out of the agreement. In 1982 it explored on its own a possible link with Grundig, but the deal was vetoed by the German cartel office in 1983. Finally it returned to J2T when it acquired Telefunken following the collapse of the parent company, AEG-Telefunken. By then, European sales of video-recorders were so high that the Berlin plant did not have enough capacity. J2T seized the opportunity to convert the videodisc plant in Newhaven to produce video-recorders (the market for videodiscs having failed to come up to expectations). Meanwhile, Thomson had signed a separate agreement with JVC to supply some of the key mechanical components needed by the J2T venture.

By all accounts, this venture has worked well. Thorn is seeking to repeat its VHS success with JVC's VHD videodisc format, although it is finding this product more difficult to establish against the competing Philips format than was the case with JVC's video-recorder. It is unlikely, however, that JVC would have a better chance of establishing the VHD format by going it alone, and in any case it seems to respect Thorn's marketing experience.

If there are strains within J2T, they would appear to stem from Thomson's activities. The fact that it entered into a separate agreement to provide components for the J2T venture was a sign that it was less than fully committed to the venture. It persuaded J2T to market a video-recorder which it had developed on its own. The impression given by the French company is that it sees collaboration with JVC as less of a permanent solution than does Thorn. It seems, therefore, that the ambitions of the European partners are changing, and this may well pose problems in relation to the future structure of this joint venture.

By most criteria, however, the venture has been successful. It is, apparently, profitable. The British and Japanese partners seem on the whole to respect each other. This is particularly true of JVC and Thorn, as one might expect, given that key figures in Thorn have been frequent visitors to Japan since the early 1970s, when it was buying products on an OEM basis. On the manufacturing side, JVC has paid Thorn the compliment of signing a long-term contract under which Thorn will manufacture up to 170,000 TV sets per annum for sale in the United Kingdom and on the Continent. It is extremely rare for a Japanese company to contract a non-Japanese competitor in the industrialized world to manufacture on its behalf. The fact that JVC and Thorn EMI have come to this arrangement shows the mutual respect which has developed between the two companies. The J2T venture clearly helped to consolidate the relationship.

The venture does not appear, however, to have led to the joint development of products in a way that other collaborations have done. JVC still leads the way when it comes to developing new products, while Thomson's research seems to be competitive rather than collaborative. Thorn EMI remains dependent on JVC for major product innovations.

The situation in the mid-1980s

Although this analysis has concentrated on collaborative cases, Japanese consumer electronics companies have in fact tended to invest directly both in the United States and in Western Europe. The bulk of Japan's European CTV investment has gone to the United Kingdom, and its VCR investment has been split primarily between Britain and Germany.

The Japanese have not been totally satisfied with their experience in Europe. Complaints about the quality of components are common. Those who defend the European electronic component companies use arguments to be heard in other sectors. They point to the difficulties of supplying components for systems designed in Japan, often to technical specifications which are not common in Europe.

Efforts are now being made to try and persuade Japanese consumer electronics companies that it would be a good idea to locate some of their design or development operations in Europe. For a short while in 1985, it looked as though Matsushita might pioneer such a development in the United Kingdom. Mr Toshihiko Yamashita, the company's president, visited Britain and on his return to Japan expressed some dissatisfaction with how the company's subsidiary was adapting its products to the UK environment. He was reported to have suggested that Matsushita should create a research centre in the United Kingdom which would include some British employees. The circumstances surrounding this alleged proposal are confused and there are no signs that it will be followed up.[59]

Some European observers argue that Japanese companies in the United Kingdom are missing opportunities by not paying sufficient attention to developments in Europe. For instance, Britain has developed a lead in teletext,[60] for which, admittedly, only a specialized market exists at present, but gradually the designs of the more expensive sets will take it into account. Japanese-designed sets, however, do not accept the relevant chip with ease, and therefore cost slightly more to convert. It is difficult to think of cases in consumer electronics in which Japanese companies have got their designs significantly out of tune with European market require-ments; when it does happen, though, it usually involves products which are developed in Japan rather than in Europe. In the related area of home computers, however, there have been cases in which Japan's reluctance to produce designs which correspond to European markets may have led to product failure. Its MSX standard, which was developed for it by the American software house Microsoft, has clearly been a failure in its current form. This suggests that the Japanese are less sure-footed when it comes to marketing more socially complex products. Given that the key to achieving success in this industry lies in the intimate relationship between software and hardware, some aspects of European software development may be more important than Japanese companies seem to think.

Philips

No European company, with the exception of Philips, appears to have the innovative ability to regain a competitive position in relation to Japan. However, even Philips still has to prove that it can take a product such as the compact disc (which it developed) and devise a way of outcompeting the Japanese opposition. With regard to video-recorders, it was forced to adopt the VHS format in preference to its own, and as far as the videodisc is concerned, it had to ask the EC Commission in Brussels for an increase in the relevant tariff almost before its own production had started.

What is notable is that Philips, the company which comes closest to being a 'European champion', has clearly decided to work much more closely with Japan and with other countries in East Asia, because it sees this region as the world's video centre. Thus, it is building video-recorder factories both in South Korea and in Japan (where the plant will be part of a video development centre).

This policy does not mean that Philips is becoming another 'hollow corporation'. The only way it will survive will be by successful product innovation, development and marketing. Indeed, it is perfectly plausible to argue that the only sure way today that a consumer electronics company such as Philips can test itself and keep abreast of trends which will later sweep the world is by establishing a viable operation in Japan. The argument that Philips's European operations (probably slimmed down) will only start to regain their competitiveness once the company manages to hold its position in East Asia is controversial, but it reflects the fact that only Philips among the relevant European companies seems to be trying to remain a world player.

Collaboration or competition?

There is very little evidence to suggest that Japanese companies need to collaborate with non-Japanese ones in consumer electronics except as a way of getting round protectionist barriers. Even then, most of them have been able to acquire 100% controlled investments. There seems to be relatively little that European or American companies have to offer them; so collaboration is not an attractive option.

Philips's apparent strategy of deepening its involvement in Japan and East Asia is a graphic illustration of the changed relationship between the Japanese industry and the rest of the world. Thirty years ago, Japanese companies had to go to foreign companies to get access to the necessary technology and marketing know-how. Today, it is the foreigners who need links with the Japanese. This is not to say that all is bleak on the European front. Developments in teletext and videotext keep Europe among the pioneers in these sectors. Its use of computers for education has been ambitious. There have been moderately innovative developments in home computing, although the potential sales of products in this area do not match those of best-selling consumer products such as the VCR. But listing such cases only highlights all the product areas where Europe remains second best.

It can be argued that failures at the level of European policy-making have played a part in weakening corporate defences. Attempts to create a new standard for satellite broadcasting services (C-MAC) with the defensive power of PAL have so far come to little. National rivalries have been partly to blame, along with the failure of countries such as the United Kingdom to formulate a coherent policy. However, the fact that Europeans are seeking new standards as a form of protection against the Japanese is significant, because it is part of wider European efforts to develop intra-

European collaboration in high-technology sectors, which, if successful, will mean the decline of collaboration with Japan.

What is now becoming apparent is how badly consumer electronics got overlooked in the first round of European collaborative research programmes, such as ESPRIT in the information technology sector and RACE in telecommunications. The mid-term appraisal of the ESPRIT programme revealed that Europe does not really have any credible long-term research in areas such as high-definition television and flat screen technologies – the kind of developments in which it is crucial to have a foothold if the industry is ever to recover. It looks as though some relevant initiatives can be expected in future versions of ESPRIT (or perhaps under the EUREKA series of initiatives). One of the first collaborative projects which won approval under the EUREKA programme was concerned with creating a common European standard for the use of computers in education – an area in which European innovation seems strong. Certainly, the whole related area of the application of computers to the home environment has moved rapidly to the forefront in the minds of European policy-makers.

So far, European countries have been extremely reluctant to involve Japanese companies in any of these projects. For example, it is understood that only those US companies with marketing, production and research capabilities within the EC are potentially eligible to participate in ESPRIT. According to this principle, most Japanese companies would be excluded, because their research capabilities in Europe remain insignificant.

In consumer electronics, then, the focus of European industrial collaboration may well be switching away from Japanese/European collaboration, to pre-competitive collaboration between European companies, the aim being to make Europe a more effective long-term competitor with Japan. On the other hand, Philips's increasing preoccupation with strengthening its presence in East Asia points to the limits of intra-European collaboration. Given that the world's most advanced market for consumer electronics products is in Japan, collaboration within Europe will lack that all-important immediate feedback from Japan's marketplace.

To look to the future, Philips and Sony seem likely to create common standards for products such as compact disc players, and this points to one important area where collaboration may develop.

Sony, for instance, has put together a worldwide group of companies to back its eight-inch camcorder format. Philips sees the setting of world standards for products and systems as an important way of achieving 'orderly competition'.[61] However, standards can be used as protective devices, and in the areas of satellite broadcasting, high-definition television and interactive home systems we may yet see some sharpening of intercontinental competition.

6

THE AUTOMOTIVE SECTOR

The automotive industry is another sector in which Japanese companies have been catching up with the global competition.[62] In terms of trade performance alone, the Japanese have moved ahead of the pack. However, their auto companies have yet to achieve the kind of dominance that has been attained in consumer electronics (where the Japanese have become product innovators). In fact, in some areas of the automotive sector, particularly luxury cars, Japan is having to struggle hard to catch up. Its competitiveness in the sector as a whole has rested heavily on production efficiency, relative currency relationships and marketing expertise.

The other general point which needs to be made is that the current structure of the Japanese industry is somewhat artificial. An excessive number of companies have been kept in the industry because protectionism in the United States and, to a lesser extent, in Western Europe has boosted the sector's profits, thus postponing the day when Toyota's dominance will drive some of the smaller players out of business.

As mentioned earlier, in the period immediately after 1945, the Japanese industry received some assistance from UK and French companies. In the early 1970s, the three American giants, Ford, Chrysler and GM, took equity stakes in Toyo Kogyo (now known as Mazda), Mitsubishi Motors and Isuzu respectively. (General Motors also bought into Suzuki in 1981.) By all accounts, the Japanese companies concerned viewed these foreign ties with a certain amount of shame, but they were financially vulnerable, and the Americans were pushing hard to get access to the Japanese market.

The first positive steps by Japanese auto companies seeking more acceptable collaborative relationships were taken in the late 1970s. The pioneering deal was a technical licensing agreement between Honda and the Austin-Rover Group in 1979 – a cooperative arrangement which has deepened with time. It was followed a year later by Nissan's equity investment in Spain's Motor Iberica and its joint venture agreement with Italy's Alfa Romeo. In 1981, Nissan

Table 6.1 Car production plants of Japanese companies in North America and Western Europe

Companies	Country	Form of investment	Planned	Start-up	Employees	Planned production
N. America						
Honda	USA	Direct	1978	1982	2,600	360,000
Nissan	USA	Direct	1980	1983	3,000	240,000*
Toyota/GM	USA	JV	1984	1984	2,500	250,000
Toyota	USA	Direct	1986	1988	3,000	200,000
Mazda	USA	Direct	1985	1987	3,500	240,000
Mitsubishi/ Chrysler	USA	JV	1985	1988	2,900	240,000
Fuji-Isuzu	USA	JV	1986	1989	1,700	240,000*
Honda	Canada	Direct	1984	1986	700	80,000
Toyota	Canada	Direct	1986	1988	1,000	50,000
Total					20,900	1,900,000
Europe						
Honda/Rover Group	UK	Licence	1979	1979	n.a.	n.a.
Nissan	UK	Direct	1984	1986	2,700	100,000
Nissan/Alfa Romeo	Italy	JV	1979	1983	n.a.	29,000†
Nissan/Motor Iberica	Spain	Acquisition	1980	1980	(Commercial vehicles)	

JV – Joint venture.   *Partly light trucks.
†Production suspended at time of writing.
Source: Japan Automobile Manufacturers' Association, Tokyo.

entered into a broad agreement with Volkswagen, and as a result began producing VW's Santana model under licence in Japan in

1984. In that same year, it also decided to make a greenfield investment in the United Kingdom.

There have also been some less well-known collaborations. Toyota, Japan's largest car company, has not yet made a major investment in Western Europe. Its only involvement has been a minority 16.5% stake in Lotus, the UK sports car and design consultancy company. Early in 1986, GM bought the rest of Lotus's equity, leaving Toyota in an exposed position. After a short while, it sold its stake to its US competitor. GM is producing through Bedford, its UK commercial vehicle subsidiary, two vans under licence from its Japanese associated companies: Isuzu's Fargo van, which is being sold as the Bedford Midi; and Suzuki's Every van, which GM has renamed the Rascal. In some European markets, Ford Europe is selling a Mazda light van as the Econovan.

At roughly the same time as they were entering into agreements in Europe, the Japanese companies turned their attention to the United States. In 1977, Honda decided to build a motorcycle plant in Ohio. It was subsequently converted into a plant for manufacturing cars and came on stream in 1982. In 1980 – a year after the imposition of a 25% tariff on imported light trucks – Nissan decided to open a plant in Tennessee (which became operational in 1983) to produce trucks, and then automobiles. Toyota played its cards more cautiously, and entered into the NUMMI joint venture with GM in 1984. A year later, it decided to go it alone and set up its own plants in Kentucky and in Canada. In 1985, Mazda decided to set up business in Michigan, and Chrysler and Mitsubishi entered into the Diamond Star manufacturing venture in Illinois.

When, at the end of the 1980s, all these North American plants are fully operational, they will be capable of producing 1.9 million vehicles per annum and will employ 21,000 people. This will give them an annual output of 91 vehicles per worker. Since in 1985 Japanese companies in Japan were producing 64 vehicles per employee, it is assumed that the North American plants will be less fully integrated than Japanese ones. In other words, they will buy in most of their components and concentrate on the assembly side of vehicle production, whereas in Japan a significantly greater proportion of components are made in-house.

In general, Japanese companies have entered into such ventures to get round protectionist barriers, though some, such as Honda and Nissan, have moved faster than others. At the same time, several of them were in fact approached by potential foreign partners, so that some of these deals are more complex than they appear at first.

Honda's collaboration with the Austin-Rover Group

Honda is an example of a medium-sized Japanese auto company (it ranked seventh in 1980) which needed to establish itself overseas in case the Japanese market turned sour. Because it had an export ratio of 69%, it was vulnerable to protectionism. It therefore decided in 1977 to start production in the United States, concentrating first on motorcycles, which did not require a large investment, and for which there was no direct US competition.

Austin-Rover's involvement with Honda resulted from an approach by the UK company under the new leadership of Michael Edwardes. Austin-Rover needed to turn its fortunes round rapidly. Its overstretched management could not develop the complete range of new models which the company badly needed, without outside help. Collaboration was called for. An American deal made no sense to the company, since Ford and GM were already its major competitors in the United Kingdom. A West European deal was excluded (although one could probably have been struck), because continental companies were interested in improving their access to the UK market, but would not give Austin-Rover rights to models which could be used to rebuild its share of continental markets. An arrangement with Honda made sense, because Honda had no established position in Europe to protect and could therefore work *with* Austin-Rover.

The initial deal was an OEM one. The Austin-Rover Group licensed a Honda model, the Ballade, for assembly as the Acclaim in the United Kingdom on a 'knockdown' basis (i.e., the bulk of the components were imported from Japan). This arrangement involved little input from the Austin-Rover Group. Honda received a licence fee, and also earned income from the provision of major components such as engines and gearboxes. Even the key machine tools were imported from Japan. The agreement worked well enough. The next Honda model (the Accord) was modified somewhat by Austin-Rover's designers so that it could be sold as the Rover 200 range. Austin-Rover engines were used in one model (the Rover 216), and Honda engines in the other (the 213).

54

The limited collaboration between the two companies grew with the joint development of the 'XX' luxury car range, which was eventually known as the Legend range by Honda, and as the Rover 800 by Austin-Rover. This 2,000cc and 2,500cc range was developed by the engineers of both companies, and the work was shared as equally as possible in order to draw on the respective strengths of the two design teams. The Honda designers were considered to be stronger in electronics and engines, while the UK team was judged to be good at interior and chassis design, and at suspension systems. The motives behind the decision to deepen collaboration revolved around the need to economize on design staff at a time when the UK company was having to replace the ageing models at the top end of its Rover range, and when Honda needed to enter the luxury car market – a sector in which Japanese companies have been weak.

By all accounts, the collaboration has worked well. Honda has probably gained more from it, since the 'XX' (Legend) venture enabled it to draw on experienced UK design staff and expand into an up-market sector in which it had previously been weak. In contrast, the Austin-Rover Group had the more modest goal of developing quality replacement models for an existing range, in order to re-enter world markets from which it had retreated during past crises.

The fact that Honda appeared to move faster than the Austin-Rover Group in getting its variant of the 'XX' into the marketplace would seem to suggest that collaboration has done little to narrow its broad lead over the UK company. This is, however, debatable, for some of the apparent time-lag can be explained by Austin-Rover's decision to produce a more complex model range. Even so, Austin-Rover managers concede that the Japanese were very efficient when it came to getting prototypes into production.

The future of the whole collaboration was clouded in the spring of 1986 by the news that Austin-Rover's management had been talking to Ford about a possible takeover. Although the proposal was rejected, the news that the UK government was willing to consider linking Austin-Rover with an American rival must have come as something of a shock to Honda. Notwithstanding this event, the underlying logic of the collaboration remains valid. The two companies are committed to further cooperation in the form of the 'YY' project, which aims to provide replacements for the smaller Maestro and Rover 200 models.

Honda and Austin-Rover are both relatively small players on the world stage. They will therefore need to collaborate with other companies to maintain a full model range. Neither company is likely to dominate the other to the extent that one of the giant American companies would if it teamed up with either of them. It is almost certain that the Austin-Rover Group would not have survived without its collaboration with Honda. However, the Group continues to make substantial losses, and there is always the possibility that its government support will falter and it will be sold to another company. At that point, Honda would have a stronger interest than most companies in acquiring and restructuring it. Given that Austin-Rover's technical capabilities have improved significantly since the late 1970s, it seems likely that Honda will want to continue to work with it – though Honda has other options in Europe which it could choose to take up.

Nissan: greenfield investments and joint ventures

Nissan is like Ford: both seem to be condemned to perpetual second place in their home market and both are active internationally. Ford has tended to lead GM at the international level, and Nissan has been forced to be adventurous outside Japan in order to make up for its domestic weakness.

Nissan first moved into Europe via a 50/50 joint venture in Italy which was instigated by Alfa Romeo. The venture was created in 1980 to produce the down-market Arna model (called the Pulsar in Japan). Nissan supplies the bodies, and Alfa the engines and transmissions. The joint venture assembles the cars and returns them to Alfa Romeo for painting and final assembly. Alfa sells the model in Italy, and both companies export independently. The venture has not proved terribly satisfactory for Nissan. Alfa was an up-market company which was unable to develop the cost structure needed to produce a model like the Arna. Although the partnership officially lasts until 1989, production of the Arna was suspended in the spring of 1986. The production of a four-wheel-drive vehicle developed by Alfa was being considered at the time of writing. Nissan sources claimed that Fiat's acquisition of Alfa should not affect the venture's future.[63]

Nissan was approached for a second time in 1980, when Massey-Ferguson asked it if it wished to acquire Massey's holdings in Spain's Motor Iberica. It decided to do so, with the intention of producing commercial vehicles in Europe. The company has, in effect, become a wholly controlled subsidiary of Nissan, which has reorganized the management and production facilities that it inherited.

A year later, Nissan entered into a broad agreement with Volkswagen, initially producing VW's Santana under licence in Japan. This agreement has allowed Nissan to widen its product line and to monitor the state of European manufacturing technology, and it has given VW the chance to increase its market share in Japan. At the same time, the two companies have been collaborating in other parts of the world. In Mexico, for example, Nissan's local plant was due to start supplying engine blocks to VW's Mexican subsidiary early in 1987.

Nissan has also worked alone, notably in the United States, where in 1984 it graduated from producing pick-up trucks to manufacturing passenger cars, and in the United Kingdom, where it started producing the Bluebird saloon in April 1986, and hopes to produce 24,000 per annum by 1987. By then, it will have decided whether to push ahead with phase two of the project, which would involve expanding capacity to 100,000 vehicles per annum.

When one tries to assess Nissan's performance overseas, one is left with a slightly confused impression. Certainly, none of the joint ventures appears to have been particularly successful. German sources, for instance, suggest that VW entered the Santana licensing deal rather hastily, and neither side seems to have been very satisfied with Santana sales in Japan (though, since these have been running at between ten and twelve thousand per annum, they do not look so bad when compared with the total number of imported automobiles – 46,000 – in 1985). The Nissan-Alfa Romeo partnership appears to be in trouble, and the Alfa management is reportedly considering whether to produce cars in competition with the joint venture.

It is still too early to give a verdict on Nissan's greenfield investments. In the United States, it has been progressing sensibly, using the experience it has gained from manufacturing pick-up trucks to move into auto assembly. By all accounts, this transition is going smoothly, and Nissan is helping to pioneer the transfer of automotive investment down to the southern states. In Europe, much will depend on how efficiently its UK plant works. Although it is not strictly a collaboration according to the European definition, its size and political visibility ensure that its success or failure will affect the fortunes of the whole Japanese business community in the United Kingdom and, probably, elsewhere in Europe.

Toyota and NUMMI

Toyota's strategy contrasts with that of Nissan, Honda and other smaller Japanese auto manufacturers. While its rivals made foreign investments, Toyota sat back in Toyota City, increased its hold on the Japanese market and continued with its very successful exporting policy. Although one gains the impression that Toyota's managers considered that their strengths lay in maximizing Japanese output, and that overseas investments would only lessen their overall efficiency, in fact, they doubted whether they could manufacture cars profitably in the United States.

This 'export-first' strategy had to give as American protectionism grew. It is generally accepted that Toyota also came under pressure from within Japan to modify its position. The company decided that it would help American carmakers that were suffering from the recession and experiencing difficulties in developing fuel-efficient small cars. Its managers believed that protectionist pressures in the USA would further intensify if American auto companies were not helped to become effective competitors again. In 1982 Toyota approached Ford, but they failed to agree terms. At roughly the same time, GM approached Toyota about a collaborative project, and the NUMMI (New United Motor Manufacturing Inc.) joint venture was the result.

This venture is based on a former GM plant in Fremont, California, and Toyota is directly responsible for production. The work-force was rehired. Only former employees were given first consideration, but seniority under the GM regime was not necessarily taken into account. Of the output, 200,000 units are to be sold as Chevrolet Novas, and 50,000 will be sold under a Toyota name. (Corolla)

Because of US anti-trust law, the collaboration had to be a limited venture. In 1985, Toyota announced that it would set up a directly owned operation. What was less expected was that GM would announce an ambitious small-car initiative (the Saturn programme) before the NUMMI venture had even gone into production. The NUMMI venture was therefore a transitional step for both partners. As far as Toyota was concerned, it was a low-risk first investment in North America. GM, for its part, got an OEM supplier of compact cars, and was able to observe Japanese management and small-car manufacturing practices at first hand. Yet the fact that GM launched its Saturn project so soon after initiating NUMMI suggests that it could have acquired the knowledge it was seeking in a more straightforward way. Unlike the Honda-Rover deal, in which learning by both sides can continue without either side being threatened, NUMMI has resulted in GM helping one of its strongest international competitors to establish itself in the United States. The two companies are condemned to compete with each other, and it is debatable which will come out of NUMMI ahead.

In contrast, Toyota has never been very interested in Europe, which it sees as plagued with chronic, unprofitable overcapacity. However, the company took a limited equity stake in the small UK specialist car producer Lotus, when the latter got into trouble in 1983. Toyota supplied parts (including engines) to Lotus, and acquired information in areas, such as suspensions, where Lotus was ahead. This limited approach to Europe left Toyota vulnerable to counter-attacks from more committed competitors. Its involvement with Lotus came to an end in 1986, when GM bought the rest of the available shares, thus putting Toyota in the untenable position of being a minority equity holder in an operation controlled by its major international competitor. It had to sell its stake to GM, thereby losing access to a source of advanced engineering design.

Other Japanese companies

Mazda and Mitsubishi both illustrate one of the basic problems that arises in collaborations: the changing balance of competitive strength between collaborating companies. For instance, Mazda and Mitsubishi originally became linked with Ford and Chrysler respectively, out of sheer financial necessity. However, by the early 1980s, the situation had changed. The Japanese companies seemed to be moving ahead of the Americans in key marketing and automotive engineering sectors. Since they could not take full advantage of their changed circumstances because they had been forced to accept voluntary export restraints (VERs), they began to think about investing in the United States on their own account. Their American partners were not very happy about this, but once the NUMMI deal had been struck, under which GM was to receive subcompact cars from what was effectively a Toyota-run operation, Ford and Chrysler accepted the inevitable. Mazda entered the United States and is to produce vehicles for both itself and Ford.

The Mazda-Ford link also shows how Japanese and non-Japanese companies can collaborate in third countries. Mazda sees the deal as a global manufacturing and distribution arrangement. It is thus supplying cars to the Ford network in Japan, Australia and other markets, while other, more complex arrangements are beginning to come into play. For example, it is granting licences to the Kia Corporation, a Korean company in which it has an 8% interest. Kia's products will be supplied to American Ford in 1988. In 1987 Mazda will supply knockdown sets to Ford Rio Ho Motor Company Ltd in Taiwan, in which Ford has a 70% stake, for supply to Ford's Canadian network.

GM seems to be creating a similar network of relationships. In addition to its NUMMI venture with Toyota, it has stakes in both Isuzu and Suzuki.[64] GM and Suzuki are developing 1,000cc cars for which there is a purchase guarantee from GM. The extension of VERs on Japanese auto exports to the United States has limited Suzuki's American sales, but it is using GM's sales network in third countries. Since 1984, Nissan has been supplying GM's Australian subsidiary with cars on an OEM basis. From 1987, GM's Korean subsidiary, Daewoo, will rely on technical licences from Isuzu and Nissan for the manufacture of commercial vehicles.

There are other cases of collaboration in third countries. As mentioned earlier, VW and Nissan are integrating their Mexican operations on a limited basis. Mercedes Benz has arrangements of this kind with both Honda (a licensing deal in South Africa involving passenger cars) and Mitsubishi. In the Mitsubishi case, MBE (Mercedes's Spanish subsidiary) is to start assembling a light van based on the Mitsubishi L3000 towards the end of 1987. Mitsubishi has been exporting cars for distribution by MBE since the spring of 1986, thus taking advantage of Spain's liberalization of Japanese car imports following its accession to the EC. Both Mercedes and Mitsubishi gain from this deal. Mercedes is widening its product line in Spain, and Mitsubishi is getting immediate access to a sales network in a country where it does not have its own.

Conclusions

The automotive sector contrasts with consumer electronics in that Japan's success so far rests less on genuine innovation than on its ability to produce competently designed products at prices which non-Japanese producers are unable to match. One of the lessons from the NUMMI venture is that the collaboration's success had less to do with advanced automation than with Toyota's superlative production management.

The automotive sector also illustrates a wider range of genuinely collaborative ventures than the other sectors under consideration. It does not just contain Japanese greenfield investments and some collaborations with foreign partners giving the Japanese access to their markets; it also includes ventures whereby non-Japanese companies have taken major equity stakes in Japanese concerns, and production arrangements in Japan for such companies as VW and the Austin-Rover Group. The range of these collaborations suggests that the sheer size and political visibility of this sector has made it special. The exertion of political pressure on the Japanese partners – both in Japan and at the non-Japanese end – is much more in evidence in the automotive sector than in consumer electronics.

The benefits of collaboration to the Japanese automotive companies have varied over time and according to the strength of the companies concerned. The smaller ones obtained financial support from larger American companies in the mid-1970s. Now, following a period in which the balance of advantages swung in favour of the Japanese, the financial strength of the American companies may be re-emerging as a major factor, given the rise in the value of the yen. The larger Japanese companies have used foreign collaborations to reduce the risks involved in establishing themselves overseas. At the same time, they have gained some direct experience of foreign luxury car design and have strengthened their knowledge in certain specialist areas. However, access to markets has clearly been the major advantage of their collaborations.

It seems that in general Japanese managements have handled their overseas operations effectively. This is certainly true of their US activities, although elsewhere, for example in Italy, there are signs

61

that, like other company managements, they can make mistakes. They now have to demonstrate that they are capable of handling labour relations in this traditionally unionized industry over a significant period of time.

The most serious challenge to the Japanese, however, comes from the fact that the automotive industry is entering a particularly fluid stage with respect to corporate relationships. Some of the current arrangements, such as NUMMI, are recognized as being temporary, limited alliances. However, companies such as Nissan and Honda may well have to decide what to do with second-ranking foreign collaborators. Should they, for example, be acquired, or jettisoned in favour of partners likely to bring more lasting benefits? There are signs that the Japanese do not yet give enough priority to such questions. As a result, they could lose out to more alert international operators – as Toyota did to GM in the case of Lotus, and Honda came close to doing when the UK government sought American solutions to the problems of the Austin-Rover Group. It may well be necessary for Japanese companies to start bidding for competitors, even if this move is not very well received by the managements of the companies concerned.

It is striking that, among the non-Japanese automotive companies, the three leading American companies are integrating their Japanese affiliates into their global strategies. Not only do the Japanese provide car models for the American networks, but the spread of joint ventures in third countries is taking the concept of collaboration between Japanese and non-Japanese companies into new territories.

Finally, among the second tier of non-Japanese companies, the Austin-Rover Group's involvement with Honda will prove a fascinating test of whether a failing company can use a collaboration not just to revitalize its product range, but to re-establish itself as a credible force in world markets – including Japan. If the Austin-Rover Group does survive – and given its dismal financial performance to date, it is by no means certain that it will – it will be a significant demonstration of the fact that collaboration with a well-chosen Japanese partner can indeed form an integral part of a long-range survival plan.

7

INFORMATION TECHNOLOGY

Japan is now predominant in consumer electronics. It is a major player in the automobile sector. But it still has to demonstrate its staying power in the general area of computing and information technology (which we take to cover semiconductors, computers and telecommunications – though we have paid less attention to this last sector).[65]

In the semiconductor industry, where the key technological developments take place, five Japanese companies are currently among the largest world suppliers, and one, NEC, was the world leader in 1985. At least part of the current success of these companies can be traced back to MITI-backed collaborative research programmes on semiconductor technology in the 1970s, one of the more successful examples of intra-Japanese collaboration. Japan has thus become a serious enough competitor in semiconductors to force the hitherto all-conquering American industry into defensive moves which culminated in the US-Japanese semiconductor accord in the summer of 1986.

In the more general computing and telecommunications sectors, Japanese companies have become major participants in their domestic market, but they still have to prove that they can repeat this success internationally. Outside observers remain highly respectful of Japan's potential. However, it is by no means certain that Japanese companies will be able to put pressure on IBM as easily as the automobile manufacturers have done on GM and others.

At first, the Japanese computer industry was highly dependent on non-Japanese companies. In 1960, fledgling Japanese mainframe producers signed a five-year basic licence agreement with IBM. This was then supplemented by a series of individual deals with specific American competitors. Hitachi signed a technical arrangement with RCA in 1961, and NEC linked up with Honeywell in 1962, Oki Electric with what became Sperry in 1963 and Toshiba with American GE in 1964. These deals gave the Japanese rapid access to the best of American computing technology and enabled them to begin to develop computers which matched IBM's models. But there were problems. Neither GE nor RCA could stand the competitive pace, and both withdrew from the computer sector during 1970–1, leaving their Japanese partners stranded. Furthermore, the Japanese companies found the arrangements too restrictive: they were not given sufficient freedom to launch the models and peripheral equipment needed by the Japanese market.

Fujitsu and Amdahl

One of the more enduring examples of industrial collaboration between Japanese and non-Japanese companies came about after this period of confusion within the Japanese industry. Fujitsu had kept clear of collaborative arrangements with the US industry, at least in part because it considered that it had an obligation to stick with the German company Siemens, with which it had historical ties.[66] However, by the beginning of the 1970s, and particularly following IBM's launch of its 370 computer series in 1971, it began thinking of switching to IBM-compatible models. At about the same time, Dr D. Amdahl, who had developed IBM's previous 360 range, set up the Amdahl Corporation, with the aim of developing mainframes which would be compatible with the new IBM 370 series.

Fujitsu approached Amdahl and an agreement was reached to set up the Fujitsu California Institute on Amdahl's premises. In December 1972, Fujitsu bought 24% of Amdahl's stock. However, events were to force the two companies even closer together. Amdahl misjudged the cost of emulating the 370 series and reached the brink of bankruptcy, at which point Fujitsu stepped forward with an offer of emergency financial aid. In the negotiations which followed, it was decided that Amdahl would scale down its production of computers, and that Fujitsu would provide part of Amdahl's range.

Table 7.1 Examples of significant industrial collaborations by Japanese companies in the computer industry

Japanese company	Country	Business partner	Year	Form of collaboration	Contents of collaboration
Fujitsu	USA	Amdahl	1972	Direct investment	OEM supply of mainframe computers' CPU, super computers and peripherals.
	W. Germany	Siemens	1978	OEM	OEM supply of mainframe computers.
			1978	Technical tie-up	Licensing of software for mainframe computers.
	UK	ICL	1981	OEM	OEM supply of mainframe computers.
			1981	Technical tie-up	Cooperation in the development of mainframe computers.
Hitachi	W. Germany	BASF	1980	OEM	OEM supply of mainframe computers.
	Italy	Olivetti	1980	OEM	OEM supply of mainframe computers.
NEC	USA	Honeywell	1984	Technical tie-up	Licensing manufacture and sale of mainframe computers and general cross-licensing on computers.
			1984	OEM	Five-year OEM supply of mainframe computers pursuant to above agreements.
	France	Groupe Bull	1984	OEM	OEM supply of mainframe computers.

OEM – Original equipment manufacture.
Compiled by Konomi Tomisawa.

The arrangement bore fruit early in 1975 when Fujitsu provided Amdahl with its (IBM-compatible) model 470V/6 on an OEM basis. Fujitsu increased its stake in Amdahl to around 49% of the equity.

The two companies work closely together, particularly in the joint development of computer systems. Amdahl takes the lead in international marketing, the collection of information and the development of new computer ranges. Fujitsu has concentrated on financing, the provision of basic technologies and the production of computers in Japan. However, their relationship involves both collaboration and competition, for the two companies compete in much of the world.

Europe

In the area of semiconductors, European companies have tended to work with American suppliers, and about 80% of the collaborative ventures in this industry are transatlantic. The most common deals have been so-called second-sourcing ones, whereby the European partners manufacture the products of American companies under licence and thus become the second supplier. Companies involved in such deals include Intel and Siemens, Zilog and SGS-Ates, and Motorola with both Thomson-CSF and Philips. Less common have been joint development and sales coordination agreements, such as the one between ATT and SGS-Ates. Philips has various arrangements with such US companies as AMD, RCA and Texas Instruments.

The involvement of European companies with the Japanese has been more restricted. Siemens has taken out licences with Toshiba, and there are production joint ventures between Siemens and Fujitsu and between Philips and Matsushita. ICL and SGS-Ates have relatively narrow deals with Fujitsu and Toshiba respectively.

Semiconductors: Toshiba and Siemens

Europe has lagged behind in the development of memory chips, which are proving to be vital, for example, in the development of submicron technology. As one of Europe's leading electronics producers, Siemens decided to make a considerable effort to catch up with the world leaders. The plan which evolved as a result of this decision brought Siemens together with the other European giant, Philips. While Siemens is to produce a one-megabit dynamic RAM chip on its own, Philips and Siemens are to work in parallel (in a 'Megaproject') to produce a static one-megabit chip (Philips taking the lead) and a dynamic four-megabit chip (Siemens taking the lead). As the joint venture will require DM 1.4 bn for R&D up until 1988 and a further DM 2.1 bn to construct three new plants, it is being subsidized on a massive scale by the German and Dutch governments, which have undertaken to provide DM 320m and Dfl 200m respectively.[67]

Siemens's one-megabit dynamic RAM chip was due to go into production in 1987. However, by the autumn of 1985, it was becoming clear that the Japanese competition would be delivering its version of this chip by 1986, thus leaving Siemens badly stranded. Although the German research ministry was financially backing Siemens's development of the chip, Siemens responded to the situation by purchasing production technology from Toshiba, the third largest semiconductor producer in Japan. The fact that Siemens ended up licensing Toshiba's production processes is yet one more piece of evidence attesting to the world lead that Japanese companies have been developing in the area of production technology.

The announcement of this collaboration caused a political row in Germany. Critics argued that, since the Siemens-Philips deal was being subsidized by German taxpayers, the licence fee agreed with the Japanese was being indirectly subsidized by the German public authorities. The Federal Research Ministry came close to withdrawing its backing for the wider Megaproject, and it has made it clear that it could still withdraw its support if Siemens were to link up with another Japanese competitor, or if the Megaproject's deadlines were to slip.[68] It now seems that it would be difficult for either Siemens or Philips to turn to the Japanese for help should the four-megabit project run into difficulties. The hostility shown to the Toshiba deal would suggest that only intra-European or, possibly, transatlantic arrangements are likely to prove acceptable to a German public which does not like the implications of its leading electronics company having fallen behind the world's best.

Fujitsu and the Europeans: Siemens and ICL

Fujitsu has done more in computing than just look across the Pacific, for in the 1970s, some years after its agreement with Amdahl, it entered into arrangements with two of the more important European players, Siemens and ICL. Both these companies have been seeking ways of surviving in the face of the dominance of IBM. In 1964, the German company had entered into an arrangement with RCA, only to be left stranded (like Hitachi) in 1971, when the

American company withdrew from computers. Siemens then helped to create the short-lived intra-European collaborative venture, Unidata, which collapsed in 1975 when the French pulled out.[69] Three years later, it switched to Fujitsu for mainframes on an OEM basis. This arrangement has worked quite smoothly as a 'long-term cooperative venture agreement'.[70] In fact, it was originally a product exchange agreement, whereby Siemens was to provide laser printers to the Japanese in compensation. But Fujitsu was apparently not particularly impressed with the performance of the Siemens printers, so it improved them and patented the results.

Siemens has been reasonably successful in selling Fujitsu computers, even in direct competition with IBM. However, it is having to compete with Amdahl, Fujitsu's US affiliate, which is marketing the same computer range. There are also signs that Siemens is no longer very happy with its role as a distributor of Japanese high-technology products, and that it is starting to try to develop more German or European-based strategies in order to lessen its dependence on Japan.

Fujitsu's original arrangement with ICL came about in 1981, when this leading UK company, which was under considerable financial pressure and about to come under new management, signed a technical assistance agreement covering the development and supply of mainframes on an OEM basis. Compared with Siemens, ICL proved pretty ineffective in marketing Fujitsu's most up-market model. However, the UK company went further than Siemens in using Fujitsu as a 'silicon foundry' in the development of its Series 39 computer range. The ICL management knew that it did not have the resources to develop a new generation of microchips on which to base its computers. By working with Fujitsu, the UK designers would be able to concentrate on the overall system architecture of their new models, and leave the advanced chip design to the Japanese, who had a substantial world lead in the emergent CMOS[71] technology. The UK systems designers are now given advanced notification of the detailed performance parameters of future generations of Fujitsu chips, to which they are therefore able to tailor their computer designs.

The ICL-Fujitsu agreement is another case of a collaboration which has deepened as time has gone by. In 1974, it was renewed for a seven-year period and expanded. As well as working with Fujitsu on another computer range, ICL has obtained an increasing amount of peripheral equipment from it, sometimes at the expense of American suppliers.

Hitachi-BASF

The cooperation between Hitachi and BASF is another example of an arrangement which goes beyond the sales cooperation of Fujitsu and Siemens. Information about this deal is hard to come by, but it is generally known that Hitachi is providing the computer know-how, and that the disc storage technology is coming from BASF. The computers are being sold under both companies' names, and BASF is doing the marketing in Europe and South America. The arrangement seems to be working well.

Other examples of collaboration

It is noticeable that most recent outward investment by Japanese companies in the general information technology area has been in the semiconductor sector. NEC has led the way. To its original investments, which it made in the United States in the early 1960s, it has added plants to produce office computers (in 1977) and semi-conductors (in 1981). In Europe, it set up a semiconductor plant in Ireland (in 1974) and one in Scotland (in 1981). Toshiba has a semiconductor investment in Braunschweig, West Germany; Fujitsu has a scattering of plants across the United States and a semiconductor plant in Ireland; and Hitachi has a broadly similar set-up, with a semiconductor plant in West Germany.

Most other activity has taken place at the OEM level. Since 1980, Hitachi has been supplying mainframes to both BASF and Olivetti. In 1984, NEC struck similar deals with the American company Honeywell and its French associate, Groupe Bull. It granted the US company the right to manufacture and sell its ACOS mainframe computers, and it signed with both companies a ten-year general cross-licence arrangement for computer developments. It also undertook to supply a minimum of 150 mainframes to Honeywell over five years.

OEM relationships are not always very satisfactory for the non-Japanese partner, because the Japanese supplier can sell the same products in direct competition to other, competing non-Japanese companies. However, there are strategies which give the non-Japanese partner better control. In some cases, Japanese machines are integrated into a system by the European company. Nixdorf, for example, integrates Matsushita products into a system which is compatible with its other computers in the medium data technology range.

The fact that firms such as Hitachi, Fujitsu and NEC have been able to offer these OEM deals is an indication that Japan's computing industry is coming of age. What still has to be proved is whether such companies can penetrate non-Japanese markets through their own independent marketing efforts. At the moment, they tend to be dependent on foreign companies for a great deal of their overseas marketing. Fujitsu, for instance, sells through Amdahl, Siemens and the Spanish firm Telefonica; it used to have a sales agreement with ICL too. Hitachi sells through National Semiconductor in the United States, BASF and, indirectly via BASF, Nixdorf. There is a possibility that Sperry may also sell Hitachi products. As mentioned earlier, NEC has sales arrangements with Honeywell and Groupe Bull.

All these deals are a tribute to the technological prowess and price competitiveness of the Japanese industry. But they also suggest that Japanese companies are still some distance away from competing globally with IBM, in the way that Toyota competes with GM or Ford. When it comes to computing equipment, the complexities of marketing are clearly much greater than in some other industries. The Japanese may eventually become the masters of computing hardware; it is less clear, however, whether they will be able to dominate the systems design and marketing end of the industry.

In fact, developments at both ends of the information technology market are difficult to interpret. In home computing, for instance, Japanese companies have been signally unsuccessful in establishing themselves in Western Europe and North America, in spite of the fact that the MSX standard for their machines was developed in collaboration with a US company. The emphasis on collaboration within the Japanese industry seems to have slowed its competitive response in a sector which punishes hesitancy. The fact that the Dutch company Philips is adopting the MSX standard for its own microcomputer range is encouraging, but there are no signs that the Japanese standard is going to be a significant challenger in the short run.

At the other end of electronics, where computing and communications interact,[72] Japan's position is also unclear. Significantly, one of the first steps taken by Japan's telecommunications utility NTT, when it was privatized in 1985, was to set up a joint venture with IBM (called Nippon Information and Communications Ltd) to specialize in telecommunications and value-added network (VAN) services. Given the importance of the link between computers and telecommunications networks, NTT's decision to work with IBM is a major blow for the Japanese competition.

The future for collaboration in information technology

Japanese limitations

In some ways, computers are more difficult to market globally than, say, television sets and automobiles. This is because they are merely the hardware part of a system which also includes a great deal of software. Products with inadequate software support simply will not sell, and here the Japanese have two severe disadvantages. First, Japan's language and its very distinctive culture mean that software developed in Japan transfers badly to other parts of the world. Second, because of the complexity of the Japanese alphabet, Japan's office automation has moved in different directions (stressing fac-simile systems) from those elsewhere in the world, where a relatively easy transition was made from the typewriter to the word processor.

The feeling one is left with is that the Japanese are having to build on their hardware strengths, which are more strictly complementary with the software strengths found elsewhere than is the case in other industries, where software is less important. Certainly, the most convincing Japanese successes in the information technology sector seem to fall into areas, such as commodity semiconductors and computer peripherals (for example, disc drives and printers), in which sheer productive ingenuity counts for a great deal. Thus, both Fujitsu collaborations seem to be based on the foreign partner's system design strengths and Fujitsu's hardware strengths. One Fujitsu manager, when commenting on the deal with ICL, suggested that his company was being used as a 'silicon foundry' – a graphic way of expressing Japan's apparent strength in this sector.

The Japanese realize that they must improve their basic con-ceptual and design skills, and they readily admit that they have much to learn from foreign sources. For instance, one of the cases in which a Japanese company is cooperating closely with a British university is NEC's involvement with researchers at Edinburgh University in the area of machine translation.

The Fifth Generation project

Japan's industry is aware that its hardware strengths will not, by themselves, be enough to bring it success in its competition with IBM, and that by the 1990s it must be capable of developing computer ranges with qualitatively new levels of user-friendliness, speed and power. Out of this awareness has sprung the Fifth Generation project, which is designed to point Japan towards the computer systems which will be required in the 1990s. It was created in 1982 and has at its core the Institute for New Computer Technology, which is known as ICOT.

From the outset the project was unusual because it emphasized the need for collaboration with non-Japanese researchers. It has in part consisted of important conferences, which have used English as the working language and have involved many leading overseas experts. At its 1984 conference, just under one-third of the papers came from Europe, and speeches were made by Brian Oakley, director of the UK's Alvey programme; Norbert Szyperski, director of GMD, West Germany's computer research organization; Jean-Marie Cadiou, director of the EC's ESPRIT programme; and David Brandin, one of the leading Americans involved in the US responses to the project.[73]

The Fifth Generation project is being allowed to proceed under unprecedented international scrutiny. It is, therefore, often cited in Japan as being a prime example of international cooperation. Foreign observers are not convinced by this claim. Despite the enthusiasm of ICOT activists, Japan's Ministry of Finance is still unwilling to hand out government money to foreigners. There has also been some confusion about whether the rights to the intellectual property arising from the project will be restricted to Japanese companies.[74]

The part that the Fifth Generation project has played in galvanizing non-Japanese governments into setting up competing programmes is fully acknowledged. Referring to a conference at which the initial proposal for the project was made, Brian Oakley has said: 'Without that conference, there would be no Alvey programme ... [it] unashamedly copies features of the Japanese programme in organization and approach.'[75] However, because the initial impact of the Japanese initiative attracted the whole of the international research community, it was at first feared that the best of the researchers outside Japan would be lured into helping Japan move ahead of the computing pack. But following the emergence of competing programmes in Western Europe and the United States, this possibility is now giving much less cause for concern. Researchers currently have a considerable range of options. The Japanese are not the only show in town.

Whatever residual reservations the West has about the Fifth Generation project, it must, in all fairness, be categorized as a significant step forward in the intellectual opening up of Japan to the outside world. Equivalent Japanese programmes in the 1960s and 1970s were closed affairs, drawing on western expertise where necessary, but specifically targeted at developing the competitive strengths of Japanese industry alone. Furthermore, the project was created amidst considerable international publicity, and this has had an important catalytic effect on world competitors. Today, the various programmes which were set up to compete with the Fifth Generation project do so in an atmosphere of openness which would have been inconceivable in earlier decades. The Japanese are taking part in a genuine intellectual debate and are open with foreigners to an unprecedented degree. There is still some uncertainty about the precise status of foreign collaborators, but this sort of tension is common in international collaborative efforts.

The European response: ESPRIT and after
It now seems that one of the most important outcomes of the Fifth Generation project has been to provoke increased European commitment to collaboration within Europe in the general area of information technology – although this development might well have occurred anyway as a response to US dominance. This defensive European response has taken the form of pre-competitive research programmes such as ESPRIT in information technology and RACE in the telecommunications sector. These programmes are designed to encourage collaboration among companies headquartered in EC member countries. Inevitably, some people have perceived them as hostile to non-European companies. US multinationals established in Europe have tried particularly hard to get access to them, and have been marginally successful.

So far, no Japanese company has attempted to join these pro-grammes, and any that did would probably be rejected. The European position is that companies can participate if they are fully integrated into Europe, carrying out a range of activities from research to manufacturing. Japanese companies are still failing to meet this criterion. Few of them escape the accusation that they are mere 'screwdriver' operations, and virtually none comes close to qualifying on the research side.

These European programmes are more than a simple response to Japanese success. They are now seen as making a positive contribu-tion to Europe's industrial competitiveness. A British official recently claimed that, whereas in the early 1980s he spent a signifi-cant amount of time encouraging UK and Japanese companies to collaborate, today the bulk of his time is spent on intra-European collaboration, and Japanese matters are now very much on the back-burner. Managers in some of the European companies involved in Japanese collaborations now speak quite forcefully about the need for intra-European collaboration. When pressed on the apparent contradictions of such a view, they argue that they are still ultimately in competition with their Japanese partners, and that collaboration with them can only act as a stopgap until the Europeans have improved their competitiveness. The Japanese are such strong competitors that European salvation must come through collaboration among relatively equal European companies. These managers are making a very clear distinction between the value of short-term collaboration as a means of strengthening the immediate product range, and the dangers of developing a long-term dependence on stronger Japanese partners. What one may therefore be seeing is a growing introversion within the European information technology community, whereby intercontinental collaboration is being replaced with intercontinental competition.

The US reaction

The response of the United States to the emergence of Japanese competition in this industry – particularly in semiconductors – has been more complex. It, too, was galvanized by reports of the Fifth Generation project. There was a growing belief that Japanese semiconductor companies had benefited a great deal from the collaborative research programmes set up by MITI in the 1970s. If those chip programmes had been so successful, what was to stop this new collaborative programme from taking Japanese industry to the top in the next generation of computing technology?

The result has been the creation of MCC (the Microelectronics and Computer Technology Corporation) in Austin, Texas. The corporation brings together twenty microelectronics and computer manufacturers (but not IBM) with the aim of developing computer architectures for non-numerical use. IBM has a similar programme under way in Yorktown Heights. It is too soon to tell how effective MCC will be, but it is a significant development, because it was given clearance under US anti-trust law on the understanding that American companies would be blown to one side unless they, too, could indulge in collaborative, pre-competitive research.

Other responses to the perceived squeeze from IBM and the emergent Japanese industry have consisted of defensive corporate mergers, such as that between Burroughs and Sperry, and a more aggressive stance towards the Japanese competition. A strident campaign against the trading practices of Japanese chipmakers culminated in a US-Japanese accord which tries to set marketing targets while putting a floor under key prices. The American industry from IBM down has also been more active in pursuing legal actions against Japanese companies which are claimed to be infringing US patents. One senses that American, as well as European, resistance to Japanese success is growing, and that this hardening of attitudes will make trans-Pacific collaboration more difficult.

Conclusions

One thing is certain about the information technology sector: international collaboration between companies will increase for some time to come. The underlying technologies are now so expensive and complex to produce that even IBM has realized that it cannot go it alone across the whole sector. Moreover, the further one moves into telecommunications, the more highly politicized marketing becomes. National monopolies are only just starting to be broken down, so that alliances, such as that between NTT and IBM or between, say, ATT and Philips, are an inevitable intermediate stage in corporate development.

Right across the spectrum, Europe is seen to be the loser. For example, in nearly all the collaborations between Japanese and

European companies, the technology and product flow is one way – from Japan to Europe. Where the Europeans do have software and systems design strengths, they do not yet seem capable of capitalizing on them, except in a defensive sense. In many ways, the US-Japanese semiconductor accord is a sign of Europe's marginal role. The Americans are more worried that Japanese companies may use Europe as a way of circumventing the accord, than they are by the fact that the European industry is an independent force in world electronics markets.

However, this is not an industry in which Japan need be pitted against the rest of the world. For instance, IBM's dominance is a worldwide problem. The emergence of the OSI (Open Systems Interconnect) standard among IBM's competitors is potentially of considerable importance throughout the 'triad' world. The fact that six Japanese companies are among the 36 suppliers of data-processing installations that have agreed to adopt this standard suggests that there are common problems which cut across continental divides.

Finally, although Japanese hardware strengths are an important fact of life in this industry, it is by no means clear that they are sufficient to ensure the competitiveness of Japanese companies. The convergence of computing and communications technologies is producing such a complex mixture of hardware and software needs that companies will probably require more than mere hardware strengths in order to survive unscathed. If this is so, then the Japanese will continue to need international collaboration. The issue for the future is what change will take place in the balance between the importance of hardware prowess and systems design strengths. It is by no means certain that systems strengths will be swept to one side, which bodes well for the stronger non-Japanese companies.

8

AEROSPACE

The aerospace sector differs markedly from the other sectors considered in this study. The Japanese are clearly dependent on non-Japanese companies, and there are no signs that they can reverse this situation even in the medium term. They must therefore follow a policy of collaboration if they are to establish themselves on the fringes of the global industry.[76]

The problem for Japanese companies is that there are major barriers to breaking into the industry. It requires massive amounts of development capital, global marketing experience and simultaneous mastery of a wide range of state-of-the-art technologies. At the same time, the domestic market in Japan is relatively small, at least in part because of the country's low level of defence spending. In the early 1980s, the Japanese aerospace industry accounted for 0.23% of GDP, compared with 0.8% in West Germany and 2.2% in the United States.

Early post-1945 developments
Japan's early attempt after World War II to break out of its position of dependence in one giant step culminated in 1967 in the YS-11, a 60-seat prop jet. The plane resulted from an intra-Japanese collaboration between the government and a consortium of Japanese companies. Mitsubishi was responsible for the final assembly. It was a technical success, but a combination of high costs and limited

world sales (182 worldwide) meant that it was not successful enough commercially to convince MITI that a purely Japanese strategy was financially viable.

The policy which therefore emerged in the early 1970s was that MITI would continue to assist R&D in this sector, but that the commercial risks should be borne by the companies concerned. This meant that they would probably have to enter into international collaborative arrangements to gain access to world markets and to the necessary project management skills. Only in the defence sector, in small commercial planes and, recently, in space has there been a significant national effort.

Japan turned its back on the cheapest option of merely buying planes from abroad. Instead, international licensing deals have been stressed, even though the production costs per plane have sometimes been twice those of direct purchase. Licensing has been used to establish Japanese companies in the technologies involved in aircraft production. However, it has proved a poor alternative to the discarded (and expensive) option of an autonomous R&D effort. It has given companies only limited experience of overall systems design, and in key technologies, such as the hot core of jet engines, they lag a decade behind their American and European competitors. Over the past fifteen years, however, a number of more important cases of collaboration have emerged.

Collaboration with Boeing

In 1973, there was an attempt to develop a 230-seat civilian transport aircraft, originally known as the YX. After initial feasibility studies, however, it was decided in 1978 to merge the project with Boeing's 767 wide-body aircraft venture. This was Boeing's first joint programme, and the company seems to have been motivated by a desire to spread the financial risk, by a need to enter the relatively nationalistic Japanese market and, more arguably, by a belief that involving its Japanese partners as subcontractors would keep them from collaborating either with other Japanese companies or in the European Airbus.[77] Boeing calls the project a 'joint programme arrangement' and has kept control of the overall design and configuration of the 767. Its Japanese partners (a consortium called the Civil Transport Development Corporation) and Italy's Aeritalia were both assigned 15% of the airframe. They also had to put up some of the initial investment (half came from MITI) and were required to assume some of the market risk.

The project has not been particularly successful commercially. Sales are running at about one-third of what had been initially projected. On the technical front, though, there have been few complaints. The Japanese have apparently performed well in airframe manufacturing, an area in which Japan's technological lag in relation to the United States is reasonably small, compared with aero-engines and avionics.

The problems for the Japanese partners of such subcontracting to share risks were graphically illustrated by the next venture in which Boeing was willing to offer them a stake. This was the project for the plane which came to be called the 7J7, and which is designed to compete with the A-320 Airbus. The Japanese were offered a larger share in the project but, early in 1985, Boeing informed them that it would slip four years and that a new prop-fan engine would be used instead of the V2500 engine, in which Japanese companies also had a stake. However, the eventual formal announcement of the 7J7 project in March 1986 revealed that the Japanese partners would be more actively involved in the programme. They obtained a 25% stake, as well as a full risk-sharing partnership, in the development, production and marketing of the plane. The indications are that Boeing views the Japanese as a useful source of funds (the Ministry of Finance is chipping in with some support) and as excellent fabricators. What is far from clear is whether this collaboration will take the Japanese partners much further towards their goal of becoming general aircraft systems designers, or even towards that of mastering the more complex subsystems such as avionics. Boeing is nevertheless giving its Japanese partners their first opportunity to be involved in the overall design of a major civilian airliner. How much they will learn from the exercise remains to be seen.

The V2500 engine

Japan's basic dependence on foreign leadership in aerospace is again evident in the engine sector. Japanese companies re-entered the engine industry after World War II by licensing designs from western companies such as Rolls-Royce. In 1979, a consortium of Japanese companies entered into a 50/50 joint venture with Rolls-Royce to produce a relatively small engine (the RJ-500). The UK company needed the development capital and was more willing to share technology than its American competitors (Pratt and Whitney, and GE).

However, the engine proved to be too small and doubts grew in Japan about the wisdom of putting complete trust in a company which had only 15% of the world market. These doubts led to an approach to Pratt and Whitney which resulted in the setting up of a particularly complicated venture to build the more complex V2500 engine. The International Aero-Engine Consortium (IAEC) was created, in which the UK and American companies each had a 30% stake, and the Japanese consortium had a 23% share. The rest was assigned to Fiat and the German company MTU.

The V2500 programme has worked smoothly, partly because it has built on the RJ-500 experience. A prototype was ready for testing within 20 months of the start of the project, and the engine will be ready for sale in 1989. Already orders have been won from Pan Am and McDonnell Douglas, although the interest of Boeing and Pratt and Whitney in the prop-fan, which competes with the V2500, raises some long-term doubts about the engine's ultimate success.

As with the Boeing ventures, we are seeing the apprenticeship of Japanese companies in an industry which is particularly demanding in terms of launch capital and the necessary combination of technologies. Japanese observers consider that their nation's participants in these projects are indeed expanding their skills. Yet, potentially, there are distinct limits to the technology transfer which takes place, since the development of planes and of engines can be divided into clear segments. This enables the project leaders to maintain control over the most demanding parts, leaving the less skilful tasks to their junior partners. In the initial stages of the Boeing 7J7 venture, for instance, the Japanese were kept well away from developments in the cockpit, which is where most of the important avionics is located. In the V2500 project, they are generally being restricted to the lower-pressure, lower-temperature parts of the engine. Since each partner controls the fabrication of its part of the engine, there is no easy way for the Japanese side to gain direct insights into the techniques used by its senior partners to produce the more complicated parts of the system.

The BK117 helicopter
Probably the collaboration that is running most smoothly, as far as the Japanese are concerned, is in helicopters. Kawasaki and Germany's MBB have produced an 8–11 seater helicopter, the BK117. The partners have shared R&D and production costs equally, and marketing is split 70/30. Kawasaki is covering Southeast Asia, most of East Asia, Oceania and the west coast of the United States. The project has been successful commercially, and the break-even point was reached in the mid-1980s. It has also been a stable collaboration which has undergone subtle production adjustments in order to maintain the required 50/50 cost split.

The reason for the project's success is that the helicopter divisions of the two companies were roughly of an equivalent size and experience; furthermore, their complementary strengths made withdrawal by either partner unlikely. Until 1980, the general direction of the programme rested with the German company but, since then, it has alternated between the two partners, and joint board meetings have been held in Tokyo, Munich, Anchorage and even at the Paris Air Show. Strong personal relations between the leading industrialists of the two companies helped the venture to succeed. Although the companies are Japanese and German, English is the working language. The time difference between the two countries also worked to the project's advantage since, by using telex and facsimile machines, the development engineers were effectively able to run double shifts.

Japan's future in the aerospace and space industries
There are few signs that Japan will reverse its policy of encouraging international collaboration in major airframe and aero-engine projects. In 1986 there were indications that the 1958 aircraft law might be revised in order to mandate international collaboration in such ventures. Even if Japan was tempted to go for a more autarchic policy, the strengthening of the yen has raised the cost of this alternative to what are probably unacceptable levels.

What Japanese companies are doing is building on their reputation as meticulous, high-quality manufacturers, and on their strengths in advanced ceramics, composite materials and electronics, in order to establish themselves as major suppliers to the world aeroindustry. However, they find their role as respected subcontractors unsatisfactory, and by accepting risk-sharing arrangements they are slowly trying to get access to the overall design process in order to establish a role for themselves which is more than that of fabricator for the world. This will involve a long hard campaign, since the aeroindustry is very compartmentalized, and the leading companies are able to control the speed of technology transfer to new entrants far more rigorously than is true in most other areas. However, the Boeing 7J7 deal would seem to be a significant step forward.

Japan does have some bargaining cards. It constitutes a significant market, so it is worthwhile for foreign suppliers to enter into collaborations which may improve their market access – though European companies have found the Japanese industry's marked propensity to buy American products an irritant. In aero-engines, for instance, there have been some questions within Rolls-Royce about whether its long involvement in collaborative ventures in Japan has really paid off commercially, given that Japan Air Lines has remained loyal to American suppliers.

Meanwhile, Japan is fully involved in satellite developments. The launch, in August 1986, of the H-1 space launcher was a further step towards the Japanese goal of developing an indigenous rocket capacity. Earlier N-I and N-II rockets were little more than modified Thor Deltas from McDonnell Douglas. However, the Japanese versions of these engines are now apparently sufficiently attractive for the American company to have decided to buy them in order to get more thrust for its Deltas. Japan's reputation is also growing in 'space peripherals', that is, the equipment that is used in parts of the industry such as ground support stations.

The H-I is significant in that it is the first launcher developed in Japan. One stage of it is predominantly Japanese and contains a Japanese engine and inertial guidance system. It is small by international standards, but a larger H-II is due for completion in the 1990s, and this one will be sufficiently indigenous to escape American restrictions preventing Japan from using launchers which are substantially dependent on US technology for launching non-government satellites. These developments are almost entirely funded by government money. The space budget has risen to about $725m per annum, which is not a massive sum, however, by international standards.

The picture, then, is of a country which is coming up fast, having set itself the goal of developing an all-round space capability, but which is still well behind the United States and Europe. Far from eschewing international collaboration, it is pushing ahead with a pressurized space module which will be its contribution to the planned US manned space station. At the time of writing, it also looks as if Japanese companies will be allowed to join the American SDI (Star Wars) programme, for which the United States badly needs to get access to a range of Japanese technologies in the area of lasers and other branches of optoelectronics.[78]

Implications for Japan's competitors

An industry such as aerospace is particularly worrying for those West Europeans who are concerned about the emergence of a US-Japanese economic axis. Japan's purchasing policies are markedly skewed towards the United States. Rolls-Royce, a European collaborator, was forced by the Japanese into accepting the additional participation of an American collaborator in the V2500 venture. Boeing has stolen a march on the European Airbus consortium by involving the fledgling Japanese fabrication industry in the Boeing programme, thus effectively preventing Euro-Japanese collaboration in airframes. On balance, this does not bode well for the European airframe industry.

There is a wider concern, though. One of the worries the non-Japanese have about Japan's interest in industrial collaboration is that the Japanese government views such collaboration as a one-way process, which is predominantly designed to strengthen Japanese corporate interests.

In the aerospace sector, in which Japan starts from a position of considerable weakness, the authorities have not been willing to sit back and let competitive logic rule, because to have done so would have meant in effect that there would not now be any Japanese companies left in either the airframe or the aero-engine business. In practice, this sector has been subsidized, and it is widely assumed that products which have a Japanese input will be given preference in purchasing programmes in Japan.

83

Aerospace

It would be unfair to Japan to use evidence from this sector to make a hostile case against its overall approach to industrial collaboration. Activities in the aerospace industry have become politicized throughout the world, so there is nothing unusual about Japan's desire to establish some indigenous capability. It is a long way from attaining the ability to develop a programme of the complexity of, say, Airbus Industrie (which, in any case, is not itself exactly a monument to the unfettered workings of economic competition). In the debate over the revision of their aircraft law, the Japanese have shown themselves to be sensitive to the costs that an autarchic policy would involve. Moreover, as long as Japan's trade surpluses are high, it will be under strong international pressure to buy aerospace products (satellites, airliners, fighter aircraft) from existing centres of excellence such as the United States and, to a lesser extent, Europe.

9

ISSUES FOR CORPORATE STRATEGISTS

When writing about industrial collaboration with Japan, it is easy to give the impression that we are dealing with something unique. For one thing, the involvement of the Japanese government might suggest that collaborations have more to do with governmental decree than with corporate self-interest. In addition, some Japanese commentators argue that there is something different about Japanese outward investment, and that the emphasis on collaboration is a distinctive Japanese contribution to the overseas investment phenomenon. We would argue, however, that Japanese companies are going through the early stages of internationalization, and that the emphasis on industrial collaboration reflects two factors: the politicized state of Japan's economic relations with the outside world in the early 1980s; and the relative inexperience of Japanese companies as multinational investors.

Japan's chronic trade surpluses led almost inevitably to an increase in protectionism against Japanese goods, which Japanese companies circumvented by investing in key end-markets in North America and Western Europe. The formation of joint ventures with local companies could often give a Japanese company a protective shield should anti-Japanese feelings be running high. Insofar as they have invested for this reason, Japanese companies are not breaking new ground. The circumvention of trade barriers was always one of the prime goals of earlier overseas investors. British and American companies, too, often used joint ventures when breaking into foreign markets.

What is distinctive about Japan's outward investment is the speed with which companies have been forced to take the multinational route. Inevitably, many of their management teams have lacked experience of the complexities of managing overseas operations. They have therefore looked for partners with the necessary local experience. Even if Japanese managements have had the necessary self-confidence, their executives will undoubtedly have been stretched by the sheer scale of the expansion required.

In these circumstances, collaboration with established foreign companies is one way of expanding which is relatively economical of scarce management skills. Thus, Honda's use of the Austin-Rover Group to penetrate the West European market enables its management to concentrate on the more important North American market. Similarly, JVC's use of European partners to manufacture video-recorders and to assemble television sets allows it to concentrate the talents of its management team on new product development rather than on managing relatively small-scale overseas plants.

There is, in fact, some statistical evidence that Japanese companies take the joint venture route more often than firms in other countries. An analysis of the ways in which the companies of nine countries entered the United States from 1978 to 1982 shows that it is rare for Japanese companies to acquire American ones. They never made more than 5% of the acquisitions in any single year during this period, in comparison with UK companies, which were responsible for 36% of acquisitions in 1982. When it comes to entering into joint ventures with American companies, the picture is reversed. Over one-third of joint ventures between American and non-American companies in the period 1981–2 involved Japanese investors.[79]

Partially owned ventures do, however, have their costs. For instance, almost by definition the expanding Japanese company will find itself working with foreign competitors which have fallen behind the best Japanese standards of performance. In many cases, the local experience brought into the collaboration by the non-Japanese company does not outweigh the problems the company brings with it. This explains why, when one looks at the statistics, the amount of strict collaboration in the non-Japanese sense involving Japanese companies is not particularly large. In fact, there is some evidence that Japanese companies are more likely than non-

Japanese companies to invest in greenfield plants when entering the United States.

One can understand some of this caution, when one thinks of Japan's past experiences of joint ventures. Many joint venture agreements were effectively forced on Japanese companies, including the Hitachi-GEC and Rank-Toshiba deals in the UK television industry. Japanese companies clearly felt hindered by what they considered to be inadequate management on the part of their foreign partners of both the technology and industrial relations. It is no wonder that, to an increasing extent, when Japanese companies have been encouraged to become involved with existing plants, they have made their willingness to take on full management responsibilities conditional on the withdrawal of the non-Japanese management and on the restructuring of labour practices. On occasion this has meant that they have in effect behaved as though the old labour force has been sacked, and they have only been willing to re-engage employees on tougher ('roll-back') terms. This has frequently been the practice of Japanese companies taking over functioning automobile plants in the United States, or television plants in the United Kingdom.

In fact, a number of the larger Japanese companies are now showing a distinct aversion to taking over existing plants, preferring to establish greenfield plants in areas which are not highly unionized. In the United States, for example, firms such as Honda have shown an increasing interest in the southern and southwestern states and, in the United Kingdom, Nissan deliberately sited its new auto plant in a part of the country (near Newcastle) which is well away from established carmaking areas. Nissan accepted the need for some kind of trade union recognition in the UK environment, but was able to create a single-union structure. This would have been virtually impossible in other, more traditional, auto-manufacturing parts of the country.

The other general observation about Japan's corporate expansion is that Japanese companies have been involved in fewer acquisitions than more established multinationals in other countries. Japan has extremely limited experience of aggressive corporate acquisitions within its domestic economy, which is in keeping with the country's horror of disunity. Given that acquisitions (particularly contested ones) are so unusual in Japan, it is hardly surprising that Japanese companies are rarely involved in them abroad.

This is not to say that there are no cases in which Japanese companies have acquired foreign ones. Within the United States, for example, Alumax took over Howmet Aluminum and Nippon Kokan KK acquired a 50% stake in National Steel. In Europe, Sony made an agreed purchase of Wega, the German audio company, in the 1970s; and Nissan gradually bought control of Motor Iberica, having initially negotiated a non-controversial transfer of a significant minority holding from the Canadian firm Massey-Ferguson. Perhaps the most far-reaching Japanese takeover of a European enterprise was Sumitomo Rubber's acquisition of a large part of Dunlop's tyre-making operations. Included in the deal was Dunlop's French subsidiary, which Sumitomo was reluctant to have. However, such acquisitions are rare, perhaps because Japanese companies are slow to react to the relatively aggressive takeover strategies of their European and American competitors.

In Europe, for instance, some eyebrows were raised at the apparent passivity with which Toyota reacted to the acquisition of Lotus by General Motors (Toyota had a minority equity stake in Lotus); at Honda's muted reaction to the controversy over the British government's apparent interest in off-loading parts of the Austin-Rover Group onto either GM or Ford; and at Nissan's restrained response to the quite prolonged negotiations in Italy over the takeover of Alfa Romeo by either Fiat or Ford. In all three cases it looked as though the Japanese companies were being outmanoeuvred by their competitors.

In fact, it is far from clear that the Japanese companies were particularly interested in these European firms. Toyota, for instance, argues that it had learnt most of what it wanted from Lotus, so that it was of little consequence if it fell into GM's hands. Honda has kept its options open in dealing with Austin-Rover by buying a factory site at Swindon. And Nissan's joint venture with Alfa had been suspended since the spring of 1986. In all three cases, therefore, the Japanese companies had reasons for responding passively. However, the fact that firms as important as Ford, General Motors and Fiat have actively been seeking to acquire the weaker European competition suggests that Japanese corporate strategies still follow a distinctive logic.

Given the fact that Japanese corporate investments in North America and Western Europe did not really pick up momentum until the late 1970s, it would be unrealistic to expect Japanese companies to be as opportunistic or as self-confident as, say, American competitors such as Ford, which have had investments in Europe since before World War I (these, too, incidentally, originally involved local equity participation). The Japanese preference for greenfield investments merely reflects the fact that this is currently the easiest way for them to exploit their undoubted advantages in areas such as production engineering, while avoiding the potentially large problems associated with their inexperience in handling foreign managerial systems. It is also natural that they, more than the equivalent-sized American or European companies, will seek to work in collaboration with foreign partners rather than acquire the foreign company. Japanese managers do not like situations of conflict, with which their non-Japanese competitors have long ago come to terms. In addition, one suspects that the consultative nature of Japanese management, in spite of its many other advantages, does not allow Japanese managers to act fast enough to counter unexpected moves by the non-Japanese competition in cases in which there is a need to block acquisitions or to take other defensive measures.

The effectiveness of collaboration

Judgments about the effectiveness of industrial collaboration are difficult to make, chiefly because observers in different countries tend to use different criteria. As the Japanese understand it, industrial collaboration aids macroeconomic adjustment and should be judged in this light. They assume that the expansion of overseas direct investment, by creating employment opportunities and accelerating the transfer of technology and know-how, makes an important contribution to the international economy. According to one recent semi-official report,[80] an annual 12% increase in cumulative direct overseas investment up to the fiscal year 2000 could reduce Japan's trade surplus by around $53 bn; but at the same time it would probably deprive 560,000 Japanese workers of employment opportunities. Although such macroeconomic calculations are debatable, this kind of investment has generally been seen as an improvement on the exporting strategy which Japanese companies have tended to favour. There is some discussion taking place between the Japanese and the rest of the world about how unquestionable a benefit this investment has generally been, and it is important that both sides recognize the inconsistencies in each other's positions.

It would probably be wrong to claim that there is universal agreement outside Japan about what counts as a benign form of direct investment. However, the level of approval tends to increase in relation to the extent that an investment introduces new products, advanced technology and improved management practices; maximizes the number of local jobs as a result of its purchasing policies; puts down research roots in the local economy; expands exports while minimizing imports – and without exacerbating any existing overcapacity; and follows a politically neutral line.

The view with which, perhaps, most would agree is that Japanese investors have generally made an innovative contribution to the industrial relations and production management of host countries. In the United Kingdom, for instance, they are seen as having prepared the way for single-union, no-strike agreements, and they introduced single-status canteens and a degree of consultation which is alien to much traditional management.[81] In most of the cases considered in this study, Japanese companies have been introducing some or all of a variety of working practices, such as 'just-in-time' inventory systems, new approaches to quality control, single-status employment, and flexible production teams. It has gradually become clear that the success of Japanese investments has often turned more on effective production management than on the extensive use of automation.

There are, however, limits to the benefits which Japanese companies bring. The further up the management scale one goes, the more dissatisfaction one finds among indigenous executives, who as a rule are not properly integrated into decision-making structures back in Japan. In addition, while managements may applaud the drive towards single-union recognition, local trade union movements are ambivalent about this development. The UAW resents the way in which firms such as Honda have managed to create non-union plants. It is also concerned by the pressure it is under to accept 'roll-back' conditions in the plants that Japanese companies have taken over from the Detroit giants.

There are also differences of opinion about the extent to which lasting transfers of technology occur in collaborative ventures. Obviously, Japanese investors take their technology and products with them when they invest overseas, and most non-Japanese accounts of Japanese plants abroad stress the high quality of production management. But there is some debate about whether these technologies are fully acquired by the local partner.

The impressions gained from a number of collaborative ventures suggest that Japanese investments provide a demonstration effect, in the sense that the local competition can no longer ignore what is being done by a Japanese management using a non-Japanese labour-force. As Japan invests abroad, the old myths about its success stemming from a cheap labour-force are being exploded. What is evident is the attention that Japanese managements give to detail and to good management practices. Non-Japanese competitors are consequently being forced into radically tightening up their own policies on quality.

However, arguments about beneficial technological and managerial spin-offs from Japanese investments can be overplayed. For one thing, many non-Japanese companies were learning lessons from their Japanese competitors when the latter were still only at the exporting stage. Company executives argue that competition from Japanese imports was sufficient to act as a catalyst, but they also tend to accept that Japanese investments have shown that Japanese management practices can in fact be successfully transferred to a non-Japanese environment.[82]

Once a Japanese company establishes its own operations overseas, the debate between the Japanese and non-Japanese about the benefits becomes sharper. The establishment of a factory is not seen in the West as bringing the automatic economic benefits which the Japanese would attribute to it. This is because different factories can make very different contributions to local economies. At the lower end of the scale, there is the 'screwdriver' operation, in which imported components are merely assembled by an unskilled labour-force. Rightly or wrongly, most Japanese factories tend to be seen as being in this category. At the upper end, however, is the factory which employs a wide range of skills, feeds off local research and development work, and uses a large number of components that are either made internally by the subsidiary or supplied by the local economy. This is the type of factory which the Japanese are accused of not setting up. As long as Japanese companies are seen as operating more at the screwdriver end of the scale, people outside Japan will not be particularly convinced by the argument that Japanese investment automatically brings major economic benefits with it.

Without making very detailed comparisons of the microeconomic performances of Japanese and non-Japanese companies, it is difficult to pass definitive judgments on this particular debate. It is true that few Japanese overseas plants come close to obtaining all their components locally. Many are currently importing over 50% of their requirements. In the NUMMI case, 60–70% of components are imported from Japan; it is only after taking labour and transportation costs into account that the domestic content of the Chevy Nova comes out at about 50%.[83] A study of 23 Japanese subsidiaries in the United Kingdom showed that, in 1982, 58% of their purchases of products for further production came from overseas – generally from Japan.[84]

However, reliable figures on local content are hard to come by. The response of one informed Japanese observer to the charge that his country's investors were merely putting down screwdriver operations was that it would be wrong to assume that all 100% investments would tend to become screwdriver subsidiaries: 'Taking VTRs as an example, close to ten companies have already begun production in the EC. While the majority of them are 100% investments, they all attained 25% local content from the startup stage and are gradually raising it. Nissan is also working earnestly in this respect . . . The gradual increase of local content is considered a natural goal by the Japanese investors. Rather than being simply compelled to do so by legal requirements, they find essential the strong promotion of supporting industries, including industrial cooperation in parts industries.'[85]

Few non-Japanese observers will find a 25% local content rate satisfactory. The EC, for instance, works on the assumption that products should have a 60% European content before they can be granted tariff-free access to the rest of Europe. In any case, definitions of local content are notoriously contentious, and opponents of inward investment will argue that most estimates of local content tend to be overstated. However, for most of the significant cases covered in this study, there are signs that plants are putting down roots to local suppliers and increasing the local content of their products. Quite often, this is being done in parallel with a significant widening in the range of their activities.

In Europe, the Nissan venture in the United Kingdom will act as a focus for this debate if the company moves into its second phase of development, and most people assume it will. At this point it will receive significant grants from the UK authorities in return for a commitment to reach an 80% local content target. The whole venture will be watched closely by established automobile manufacturers, who are concerned that Nissan is adding capacity to an industry already plagued by overcapacity. Any wavering by the Japanese company in its efforts to attain the 80% target, which has already been denounced by competitors as being too loosely defined, will be quickly publicized. For the moment, Nissan's claim that it has reached the 40% level in its first phase of investment is being received politely by the UK components industry. The main test is yet to come.

There is, however, the secondary question of the extent to which the components purchased come from genuinely indigenous companies or from the subsidiaries of Japanese component manufacturers. This is another area in which there is a perception gap between the two sides of the debate. The Japanese literature rarely raises the question of nationality of ownership, whereas western observers tend to argue that a Japanese plant which draws its components from satellite plants owned by other Japanese companies makes a much smaller contribution to international restructuring than one which buys its components locally from indigenous suppliers.

The issues here are complex. There are strong reasons why companies going overseas will tend to encourage their traditional suppliers to go with them. Technical specifications, for instance, vary from country to country, and it takes time for local component suppliers to come to terms with non-traditional specifications. In addition, the first wave of Japanese overseas investments has been on a relatively small scale; the plants have not been the source of so much business that local companies have felt strongly motivated to bid for it. Japanese assembly companies certainly do have particularly strong corporate ties with Japanese components suppliers, but as mentioned above, this has been a problem when companies from other nations have invested abroad. At the same time, the economic problems of supplying components to small-scale assembly operations hold a number of Japanese components suppliers back.

In the meantime, Japanese companies are clustering around certain key ventures. In the United Kingdom, Nissan has been insisting on, and sometimes arranging, Japanese partners for many of the local contractors.[86] Inevitably, local components suppliers are concerned, even though a link with a strong Japanese partner could open up opportunities to supply some components to Japan, however small the volumes might be initially.

Japanese companies are becoming aware of the worries this tendency is causing. Recently, for example, when US journalists were claiming that Toyota would be bringing ten to twelve affiliated components suppliers with it for its new plant in Kentucky, Toyota replied that it was only bringing three: Nippondenso, Aishin Seiki and Toyoda Gosei. In particular, Toyota maintains that it will not try to replicate Toyota City in the United States; in other words, it will not encourage components companies to locate themselves near its assembly plant. Nippondenso and the others will thus build their factories in states other than Kentucky. Toyota claims that any of its other traditional suppliers in Japan that go to the USA will be acting independently.

The Japanese case is currently weakest in the area of research, development and design facilities. Some of the problems to do with components stem from the fact that RD&D still tends to be located back in Japan. A non-Japanese components supplier, no matter how good it is, will be handicapped if it cannot start work on a particular item until Japanese designers have finalized designs in Japan. Components companies and product designers increasingly work hand in hand, but this is difficult if the design is being done on the other side of the globe.

To some extent, those who criticize Japanese companies overstate their case. Only a handful of multinationals of the stature of IBM have in fact created a chain of research centres around the (generally industrialized) world. Japanese multinational companies are still wrestling with the problem of setting up and managing their first major wave of overseas manufacturing plants. It is unrealistic, therefore, to expect them to have had the time to establish the research facilities which would anchor their plants more closely in the local economy.

Japanese managers do not appear, however, to be particularly sensitive to demands that they increase the amount of research done overseas. In the course of our study, NEC managers were the only ones who responded positively to this question. They explained that they were already establishing links with foreign academics (particularly in Scotland), and accepted that overseas research could draw on distinctive foreign strengths which would help Japanese companies develop products that were more finely attuned to end-markets. In general, though, interviews and secondary sources provided no convincing evidence that the bulk of Japanese managers in electronics and automobiles consider that they have much to gain from establishing research laboratories outside Japan. There is a limited amount of design work being done overseas: the German end of Sony-Wega has been given some freedom to develop its own designs; Hitachi in the United Kingdom has a product design department with some twenty employees;[87] other firms have announced that they intend to boost their overseas design and development activities, but action is still limited.

Some Japanese may not consider that this matters, but there is a tendency in Europe at least to see the establishment of research activities as the ultimate test of whether a company is a good corporate citizen. Established American multinationals in Europe argue that their operations, in contrast with those of Japanese newcomers, are often fully integrated, in that they carry out the whole chain of corporate activities from research onwards. It is widely acknowledged that only properly integrated foreign companies will be allowed to participate in European high-technology initiatives. At the moment, Japanese companies are excluding themselves.

However, when all the pros and cons have been assessed, one major fact deserves some comment. Japanese companies are very recent investors in the industrialized world. This inevitably makes them cautious. It is therefore totally unreasonable to level the complaint against them that they have not integrated themselves as closely into host economies as the more established multinationals have in Europe and the United States. All one can ask of them for the moment is that they acknowledge that screwdriver operations are only acceptable as a provisional first step in the process of becoming a fully fledged multinational. The evidence suggests that most Japanese investors are increasing their foreign involvement, partly out of choice and partly because foreign authorities are setting them targets. They will deserve condemnation if they do not continue to make progress in putting down deeper foreign roots. In

95

the meantime, however, they are bound to make some initial mistakes. They deserve some understanding.

Collaboration and competition with Japanese companies

Given Japan's tendency to run trade surpluses and the resulting rise in protectionism and in the value of the yen, Japanese companies are having to invest overseas because a Japanese-based exporting strategy is becoming more difficult to sustain both economically and politically. The issues for Japanese companies are therefore primarily about whether they should invest directly abroad or enter into the kind of ventures involving foreign companies which the non-Japanese define as collaboration. These issues are not qualitatively different from those facing any would-be multinational company. The major difference is that the pressures on Japanese companies are very strong, so that they are having to move very fast by the standards of older multinational companies.

However, the problems facing non-Japanese companies that are given the opportunity to work with their Japanese competitors are more complex. The fact that Japanese companies are having to move so fast is a tribute to their redoubtable competitive strengths. This raises the question of whether non-Japanese companies can work with their Japanese counterparts without being destroyed in the process. This question must be faced, since there is a considerable body of hostile opinion in the United States and in Europe which argues that Japanese companies are unreliable partners.[88] Is collaboration the thin end of the wedge, whereby Japanese companies work with and then discard local partners? Or are there ways in which collaboration can be used to absorb the first shock of Japanese competition and develop long-lasting mutually acceptable relationships?

There have in fact been very few cases in which a serious non-Japanese partner has been unceremoniously pushed aside and supplanted by its Japanese collaborator. The cases which come closest to demonstrating this kind of behaviour are the Fujitsu and Amdahl venture, in which the American company has become little more than a marketing arm for the Japanese firm, and the GEC-Hitachi and Rank-Toshiba joint ventures, in which the two UK television manufacturers were soon jettisoned. Another source of complaints concerns local companies that have signed OEM deals with Japanese companies only to find that their Japanese partners are competing independently.

However, none of these cases has involved anything very exceptionable. In the Fujitsu-Amdahl case, the American company was from the beginning the untested force which had to establish itself as a new competitor against IBM, and as it ran into trouble, Fujitsu was forced into taking a greater equity stake. As for the UK cases, no one seriously argues that the British partners would have remained in the television industry anyway. So these interludes with Japanese partners were no more than that – a transitional period of no real importance. The OEM cases raise little sympathy for the non-Japanese companies. After all, a western company turns to a Japanese firm because this firm makes a particular product more effectively than it does. Unless the western company revitalizes itself rapidly, it is inevitably vulnerable to competition from the Japanese company. An OEM deal barely counts as collaboration, and it is therefore unrealistic to think of it as imposing any particular obligations on the supplier.

If western critics really want to argue that Japanese companies are absolutely ruthless competitors, the evidence has to be sought in areas which are tangential to industrial collaboration. There are those in the American semiconductor and computing industries who make charges of this kind, but most of their complaints are really about the alleged unfairness of help from the Japanese government (the 'targeted intervention' issue), and about pricing strategies (which gave rise to a classic dumping problem).

The semiconductor industry is a highly competitive sector in which Japanese and American companies see themselves as locked in a life-or-death struggle. It is not surprising, therefore, if there are tensions. However, these tensions are not particularly related to the industrial collaboration side of the partnership, although some of IBM's disputes with Japanese companies have turned around differing perceptions of the licensing relationship.[89] Given that licensing is one element in the spectrum of collaborative activities, these disputes are relevant to the debate. However, it has to be admitted that the Japanese and non-Japanese members of our team found it difficult to agree a common interpretation of them.

It is easy to feel some sympathy for Texas Instruments, which has just been supplanted by NEC as the leading semiconductor producer in the world. When it applied to enter the Japanese market two decades ago, it was kept waiting for two and a half years for MITI approval. It was then forced to enter into a joint venture with a local company (Sony), to license its basic patents on semiconductors to the Japanese opposition, and to restrict its initial production in order to give local rivals a chance to catch up.[90]

These tough Japanese tactics did not seem to matter too much then, but times have changed. From the welter of charges and countercharges that the American and Japanese semiconductor industries have been throwing at each other more recently, two main points emerge. First, American semiconductor companies, which as a group have made the most serious attempt to penetrate Japanese markets by investing there, have been particularly virulent in their complaints about the lack of openness of these markets. Second, the countersuit filed by NEC against an American company (Texas Instruments Japan, as it happens) alleging infringements of its own, Japanese, patents indicates how the technological balance of power within this key industry is moving (whatever the legal merits of NEC's case). Complaints about the trade implications of Japan's industrial policies will doubtless continue, but there is a new dimension to the debate now that Japanese technology shows signs of surpassing western achievements in certain important sectors.

Most other industries have experienced a rather deeper level of collaboration than semiconductors, and the picture is therefore different. The majority of the main collaborations are in their second or third phase, and the partners are working together on a wider range of activities. This is certainly true of the Austin-Rover Group and Honda, JVC and Thorn, JVC and Thomson, ICL and Fujitsu, and Fujitsu and Amdahl. Even if Japanese motives are different in the aerospace sector, the same picture emerges from both Rolls-Royce's and Boeing's relationships with their Japanese partners. These collaborative relationships would not be deepening if one partner considered that the other was aiming to destroy it.

It is certainly not the case that only non-Japanese partners need worry that collaboration may ultimately reduce their competitiveness. In the Boeing airframe collaborations, for instance, the Japanese seem to be in a dependent position, and there is little sign that Boeing will let this situation change.

The GM-Toyota relationship illustrates that, even if companies are reasonably happy with the way a collaboration is going, at some point each partner has to make an assessment of what is likely to become of the long-term competitive relationship. A collaboration that is likely to lead to a merger between the companies involved is clearly very different from a purely short-term, tactical alliance between companies that see themselves ultimately as competitors. The more complicated the collaboration, the more important it is, if tension is to be avoided, that each company takes great care when it comes to deciding what its strategic goals are in entering into such an agreement.

The ambiguities at work were well illustrated in a speech given recently by a senior manager of a European company which is collaborating with a Japanese competitor. He spoke about the need for European firms in his company's field to work much more closely with each other in order to catch up with the Japanese. When he was questioned about the apparent inconsistency in his position, he replied that his company was collaborating with a Japanese firm for short-term tactical reasons, but that, in the medium term, the two companies were competitors. His company would manage to get itself into shape towards the end of the 1990s only by cooperating with other European companies. Collaboration with Japanese firms would not produce a long-term solution to his company's needs.

Similar views are expressed by other (although not all) managers involved in collaborative programmes. The options open to European companies have been growing as the pan-European initiatives in high-technology sectors have proliferated. Programmes such as ESPRIT, RACE and EUREKA rest on the assumption that intra-European collaboration is a desirable strategy for European companies.[91] However, at the strictly corporate level, it is by no means certain that intra-European collaboration automatically provides all the answers. For instance, from the Austin-Rover Group's point of view at the time of writing, European partners are generally unattractive. They tend to be significantly larger than the UK company. Given the overcapacity in the European auto industry, this means that a European partnership would almost inevitably be at the expense of the Austin-Rover Group's own European ambitions. Whatever the company's ultimate relationship with Honda may be, at least it gives the Austin-Rover Group sufficient freedom to strengthen its position in its natural markets in neighbouring Western Europe.

This argument demonstrates the difficulties involved in passing judgments on the merits and demerits of a phenomenon as complex as industrial collaboration. Every company starts from a unique position as regards the Japanese and European competition, and judgments have to take this into account. Nevertheless, this study suggests that there are very good reasons why some European and North American companies might wish to collaborate with their Japanese competitors. Sometimes they are very short-term, often corresponding to the need to fill a particular gap in the current product range. In other cases, collaboration may bring long-term competitive gains, particularly if the Japanese company is roughly of the same size, and has complementary strengths.

Certainly, American arguments that collaboration inevitably creates 'hollow corporations' in the West – which surrender key initiatives to their Japanese partners, and thus become their tools – are not convincing.[92] First, there are cases in which non-Japanese companies would probably not have survived if they had not started collaborating with Japanese companies (Austin-Rover and ICL in the United Kingdom). Second, these arguments probably underestimate the competitive fillip given to a company, such as GM, as a result of seeing what a competitor can achieve with one of its old plants. Third, the 'hollow corporations' analysis ignores the positive ways in which companies can strengthen themselves by working with Japanese partners in mutually beneficial areas, such as the creation of joint standards.

Furthermore, there may well be cases in which ultimately healthier world competition would emerge if non-Japanese companies were to find Japanese partners rather than form alliances with competitors in Europe or the United States. This is, admittedly, a controversial argument, but one explanation for 'Euro-sclerosis' states that residual nationalism is responsible for the dearth of competition between European companies across national boundaries. It is a matter of judgment whether encouraging intra-European collaboration will quicken the pace of competition within Europe. There can, however, be few doubts that collaboration between Japanese and non-Japanese companies has generally strengthened competition in both Europe and the United States. There is, therefore, no prima facie case for arguing, on competitive grounds, that collaboration between non-Japanese and Japanese companies is any less desirable than intra-European collaboration.

Finally, without disguising the fact that Japanese companies are run highly competitively, there is no evidence in this study to suggest that the Japanese are more dangerous as partners than other nationalities. In many ways, once cultural and linguistic barriers have been breached, the reverse may well be true. For one thing, the absence of a tradition of opportunistic acquisitions reduces the possibility that collaboration will lead to unwanted takeover bids. For another, just as the Japanese have a tradition of working with a family of companies, so there are signs that they will stick by non-Japanese companies with which they have a working relationship. Sometimes, as is the case in the Fujitsu-Siemens relationship, Japanese managements are motivated by loyalties which are rooted in events predating World War II.

We would strengthen this argument by suggesting that many of the worries about collaboration with Japanese companies stem from the speed with which they have had to emerge from an extremely inward-looking industrial culture to start becoming responsible actors on the world stage. As they become more experienced in working with other cultures the problems will decrease. In the meantime, for alert non-Japanese companies, Japan offers opportunities as well as competition. Collaboration with Japanese companies is one strategy now on offer. In some cases, it can provide a very attractive solution to a company's strategic problems. This does not mean that the companies concerned will stop competing. To quote the conclusions of a UK executive who has been closely involved in Austin-Rover's link with Honda, 'Japan, competition or collaboration? No, Japan, competition and collaboration.'[93]

10

ISSUES FOR GOVERNMENTS

The Japanese

For Japanese companies, outward expansion is no longer optional. Given the rise of the yen to levels which make many traditional exports unprofitable, either they will have to discover radically new investment strategies in order to capitalize on restructured domestic markets, or, more likely, they will need to find foreign production bases to replace their export-from-Japan strategies.

The Japanese authorities will legitimately continue to stress the macroeconomic benefits of an extension of Japanese outward investment, in whatever form it takes. As the surpluses in key bilateral trading relationships respond to a stronger yen, one can expect some of the pressures against Japan to weaken. On the other hand, the industrial adjustment which is helped by outward Japanese investment is now more likely to be called for within the Japanese economy itself. So far, few of the ventures discussed in this study have involved job losses or drastically reduced profits at the Japanese end. This situation may now be changing. Under a strong yen regime, outward investments may increasingly be at the expense of Japanese plants. The quite wide belief among the Japanese in the benign workings of macroeconomic forces may be about to face its severest test.

So, what does this mean in direct political terms for the Japanese government?

First, its diplomatic priorities will need fairly rapidly to switch from the trade politics that have been so central in the past decade to fostering the wave of Japanese investment that is likely to be seen over the next three or four years. Everything must be done to ensure that the most visible projects of the initial wave of Japanese investments (particularly the automobile investments in the United States and Europe) go smoothly, without running into any controversies. Nearly all official and semi-official Japanese policy statements now routinely stress the benefits of international collaboration, so we are really talking of a continuation of current policies, with some extra attention to the sensibilities of the host countries. Such proposals as the one for the establishment of a Japan/EC Industrial Cooperation Centre could marginally speed up the acceptance of Japanese management practices. In addition, there should be growing emphasis on developing local research, development or design units, and on monitoring local content ratios.

Second, the Japanese authorities will want to ensure that Japanese companies abroad come to be treated as local companies as soon as possible. This may take a bit of time to achieve, but, at the very least, the authorities can monitor activities such as foreign public purchasing policies to see whether they are being opened to Japanese companies as these become an increasingly integrated part of the local economy.

Third, the Japanese will need to encourage collaborations which increase exports from the host economies. They should welcome complex relationships, such as those now found in the automobile industry, which involve Japanese and non-Japanese competitors in third economies such as South Korea and Taiwan. If a strengthened yen rules out certain investments within Japan, then every encouragement should be given to collaborations within the immediate region, even if these are apparently at the short-term expense of Japanese jobs.

Finally, the Japanese authorities will need to come to terms with the growing foreign insistence that the overseas expansion of Japanese companies is matched by an increased encouragement of foreign companies into Japan itself.

A number of measures have already been taken to encourage such a reverse flow of trade and investments. MITI, in particular, is now using its JETRO[94] offshoots to promote, among other things, foreign investment into Japan rather than Japanese exports. There are various schemes in place to help foreigners identify Japanese partners, speed the processing of investment applications, and provide loans to the inward investor. MITI has gone further by starting to invite representative foreign managers to some meetings of its advisory committees, such as the Trade Council, Goods Import Council and the joint planning committee of the Industrial Structure and Industrial Technology Councils. Such committees are at the heart of the consultative networks which surround MITI, and the fact that foreign executives are being given some access to them is a significant step forward.[95]

The trouble is that foreign investors continue to find Japan a difficult environment, not really because of political harassment, but because of all the embedded institutional and cultural barriers that make the Japanese economy a very much more complex investment site than, say, the United States is for a European investor. The problem for the Japanese authorities is that, although those foreign companies that have seriously tried to invest in Japan are generally quite understanding,[96] many decision-makers in Europe and the United States are not. Americans, in particular, still often believe that Japanese economic success is the result of determined intervention by the Japanese government. Westerners, in general, continue to attribute the difficulties non-Japanese companies have in expanding their operations in Japan to obstructionist Japanese policies.

Such an interpretation is clearly ungenerous to many policy initiatives that have been made in Japan. The same people in the West tend to believe that when Japanese officials talk of industrial collaboration, they have in mind only the outward expansion of Japanese companies and have not really come to terms with the fact that a genuinely two-way flow of investment will lead to some Japanese companies being swallowed up by foreign ones, or at least to collaborations where the Japanese company is likely to remain in a subordinate position.

In an era in which Japanese outward investment is going to be so dominant, it is important that the Japanese authorities should be careful to ensure that their welcome to the smaller flows of inward investment is genuine. In many areas, there is probably not a great deal more they can do to welcome foreign investors. In the financial services sector, however, there is a strong feeling in both Europe and the United States that Japan does not offer as much freedom to foreign financial companies as Japanese companies are offered in, say, London and New York.

It may seem unfair to the Japanese that developments in financial services may affect the warmth of welcome received by Japanese manufacturing companies, but this is a fact of life. Since many non-Japanese doubt whether Japanese officials regard 'industrial collaboration' as a genuinely two-way process, the warmth with which non-Japanese companies are received once they start threatening established Japanese interests will be monitored, and the results will influence how some Japanese companies are received elsewhere in the world.

The non-Japanese

Non-Japanese official thinking will have to come to terms with a new world in which Japanese multinational investment is a major economic phenomenon. Unlike investment in the 1970s, this new brand will be motivated by much more than the negative need to get round protectionist barriers. On the whole, the new wave of inward investment will come to North America and Western Europe because this is the economically rational strategy for Japanese companies to follow. Many of these companies will be relatively inexperienced foreign investors, but many others will have their own product or production engineering skills. The non-Japanese world should respond positively to such investment. As long as the yen remains at reasonably strong levels, a surge in foreign investment by Japanese companies should be accepted as a natural adjustment to Japanese economic success.

Western adaptation to Japanese investment will not, however, be without its strains. The Japanese business community is being forced to travel the 'multinational company' route at an unprecedentedly fast rate. In the case of American companies, some fifty or sixty years elapsed between the first transatlantic investment boom around the turn of the century and the investment boom of the 1960s, when the fashion for overseas investment spread to the tier of second-ranking companies below the long-established international giants. In the case of the Japanese, it is barely ten years since the first significant investments were made in North America and Western Europe, and yet we are already talking about an investment wave from Japan which will involve the kinds of company (components suppliers, leading provincial companies, etc.) which in the American case took so long to cross the ocean.

In other words, there may well be strains connected with the sectoral bunching of this investment, and with its concentration in industrial sectors in which the Japanese have already been successful in establishing export markets. As relatively inexperienced overseas managers, these secondary Japanese investors may tend to stick together, and there may be initial problems of integrating them into local economies. On the other hand, the strengthening yen will make an over-reliance on imported components from Japan increasingly uneconomic.

There will thus be a case for host government authorities to concentrate for a while on such technical matters as local contents requirements. More informally, they might encourage the Japanese companies to locate their regional headquarters or some of their R&D activities locally. This would be part of a strategy designed to encourage the Japanese investors to put down strong roots in the local economy – to the ultimate benefit of both parties.

This wave of Japanese investment will reopen a number of debates to do with inward investment in general rather than with Japanese investment *per se*. These debates are not about whether inward investment is desirable in its own right – it is now generally accepted that it is – but about how much encouragement should be given to the whole process when domestic suppliers are already in place with established spare capacity. In most countries, the inward investor is able to take full advantage of subsidies designed to achieve social goals such as the development of depressed regions, while longer-established domestic competitors, with existing plant, are often handicapped because normally only new investments attract such subsidies. The alert, internationally mobile investor has increasingly been able to use the 'dowry-chasing' game to play off local and national governments against each other, with the result that it is the public authorities that provide a good part of the initial investment in any new foreign operation. This gives the inward investor a head start over the local competition.

This is, of course, an old debate, not specifically concerned with the Japanese. However, the speed with which the Japanese business community is being forced to invest abroad, allied to the fact that most companies have no pre-existing investment ties with any particular country or region, means that the danger of host authorities overbidding for this investment is quite high.

Obviously, a few key investment projects will be of such size and prestige that it will be very difficult to restrain the competitive instincts of national or state authorities. The first Toyota factory to be located in Europe would be one such prize. It should, however, be possible to exercise some restraint on the wave of secondary investment, which can be expected in both Western Europe and North America. Bodies like the EC Commission should intensify their existing monitoring of the incentive packages which the EC member states are offering. In the USA, it may prove difficult to curb the enthusiasm of state governments; the problem of overbidding for inward investment already exists. Nor is it just an American problem, but a transatlantic one, with Scottish officials, for instance, now finding that their strongest competitors for attracting certain inward investors are not other European countries, but American states.

This kind of issue may currently seem remote to the Japanese, but it is one which, like the over-enthusiastic use of export credits, has the potential to erupt into trade disputes, which in turn can quite arbitrarily affect inward investment. For the moment, this is no more than a warning, but there are signs that there could be trade retaliation against major plants which locate in countries or states that are seen to offer too generous incentives, or that fail to demand certain safeguards.

Obviously, given the cultural background from which the Japanese companies and their managers come, the first generation of Japanese investors is likely to generate some distinctive political issues. Certainly, the managers in question are likely to be imbued with a sense of Japanese nationalism which is stronger than the equivalent nationalism found in the overseas subsidiaries of European and American multinationals. However, the monolithic position of the Japanese investors can be expected to erode quite fast. Already one can identify companies – Sony, NEC, Matsushita – which started to invest abroad out of strategic choice rather than sheer compulsion. Already one can sense that certain Japanese companies are more interested in particular European countries than others. Already, personal relationships between Japanese and non-Japanese decision-makers can be shown to have swung certain investments in one direction rather than another.

As Japanese companies prove more or less successful in different geographical locations, as their relationships with non-Japanese customers and components suppliers evolve, and as they employ a growing proportion of local managers, their investment interests are likely to diverge quite rapidly. In these circumstances, American and European industrial policies should aim to speed the process whereby Japanese companies become as internationalist in their strategies as many longer-established foreign investors. Given that Japanese companies have certain desirable competitive strengths, priority should be given to encouraging the more pliant Japanese companies in this respect. Once it becomes clear that key Japanese companies are winning greater local acceptance because they have put down genuinely deep roots into the local society, the more ethnocentric Japanese investors will follow suit. However, if no attempt is made to distinguish between the more and the less adaptable Japanese companies, and if the former win no real credit for their adaptability, then the Japanese business community will become alienated, and will have no incentive to move in directions which the Europeans and Americans would prefer.

At the moment, these fledgling Japanese investors still have to demonstrate by actions, rather than noble statements, that they are genuinely committed to revitalizing the economies of the non-Japanese world. They need to show that they intend to increase the local content of overseas plants, to create significant foreign R&D centres and to use indigenous executives far more creatively than they currently do. As will be plain from this study, Japanese companies still have a long way to go before they become as economically and socially integrated into host societies as older multinational companies are, but, equally, there is nothing in this study to suggest that they will not move fast in the recommended directions. Individual non-Japanese companies will speed this process up, and there is every reason for governments to give them firm support.

The West Europeans, in particular, have some delicate decisions to take. The growing emphasis on intra-European collaborative programmes reflects a certain consensus about the need for an industrial strategy that will allow Europe to make up some of the ground it has lost to the United States and, of course, Japan. To oversimplify slightly, the dominant position in recent years has been to favour some resort to trade barriers in those areas where Japanese competition is felt to be too strong. This approach has been allied to the development of collaborative research-oriented programmes like ESPRIT, EUREKA and RACE, which mainly involve European-owned companies.

The trouble is that a consensus which originally emerged to counter a trade threat from Japan must now come to terms with an era in which Japanese investment is going to be a major factor in the European economy. There is a danger that the current thrust of European industrial policies, with their stress on intra-European collaboration, will create in the Japanese newcomers a ghetto mentality, which will reinforce the nationalism of their approach to Europe.

By resorting to trade barriers and by encouraging the rise in the value of the yen, Europe and the United States have implicitly made a choice: if Japan is to be prevented from exporting at past volumes, then Japanese companies will need to invest overseas in order to exploit their genuine competitive strengths in key industries. The political costs of Europe and the United States launching a campaign to roll back Japanese outward investment as well as Japanese exports would be so great in terms of Japanese resentment that such a campaign is effectively not an option. Japanese investment has therefore to be accepted – with the proviso that the opening of the Japanese economy to reciprocal investment continues to gather pace.

However, such acceptance will not be comfortable for western industrialists and policy-makers. On the one hand, greenfield investments will add to overcapacity in a number of industries, thus adding to the pressures on a number of vulnerable national champions. On the other, if the Japanese investment comes in the form of acquisitions of existing European companies, the political temperature will rise, since the political culture in most European countries is not such as to allow policy-makers to acquiesce in a Japanese acquisition of a significant European champion. (After all, there are still occasional outbursts of resistance to such bids from Americans, and even from other Europeans). Even if outright acquisitions remain rare, the steady arrival of Japanese investors will continue to put pressure on European competitors, while one of the key defensive tools available to European policy-makers – trade barriers – will become irrelevant in this new competitive environment.

The next wave of Japanese inward investment is likely to have an important catalytic effect on European and American companies in Western Europe, in that they will probably step up defensive cross-frontier mergers in order to rationalize existing capacity before it can fall into Japanese hands. Certainly, established American multinationals will be an important part of this defensive strategy, and there are already signs that firms such as Ford and General Motors are taking strategic decisions in anticipation of the increased competition they expect to face.

There is thus a possibility that Europe's industrial structure will be polarized for a while between Japanese-owned or -linked companies and the rest. The temptation for the European authorities will be to develop their existing collaborative research programmes to support the emerging 'European champions', but this will become harder and harder to justify as the Japanese investment community continues to put down roots. It may still be possible to continue subsidizing some of the research of the European champions; the danger is that disproportionate sums will be spent in propping up the least efficient of these companies. On the other hand, unless European companies can somehow or other rediscover the technological dynamism to make the Japanese companies irrelevant, there will be a strong temptation for the bolder national governments to seek to integrate Japanese investors into their overall strategy, in the hope of taking the lead over those European nations that stick with purely European solutions.

The lessons which the more alert European governments will learn is that a continent-wide industrial policy which excludes Japanese-owned companies is simply too broad-brush to be viable. An industrial policy cannot work nowadays unless it creates companies capable of competing globally. This will almost certainly involve creating links with companies from all over the world, the exact pattern of linkages depending on the precise combination of technological, marketing and geographical strengths that each company can bring to a collaboration.

One can understand why European policy-makers may be cautious about accepting the new Japanese companies, which come from a business culture with an acute sense of national purpose. But we have found no evidence in this study that Japanese companies, or the authorities behind them, have any sinister motives for their emphasis on industrial collaboration. There are perfectly straight-forward economic pressures leading them to invest overseas. Yes, many Japanese companies will remain potent global competitors, playing to rules that sometimes seem alien to the West. Yes, the authorities have seen industrial collaboration as one way of buying off protectionist measures in the United States and Europe. Yes, western companies will need to be wary as Japanese companies invest directly or enter into more subtle forms of collaboration with local companies.

On the other hand, in contrast with commonly held views in the West, many Japanese observers are not particularly confident that their companies will sweep away all before them as multinational investors. The national cohesion that has been such an important factor in Japan's economic success will actually be a disadvantage as its companies move into new, very alien, business cultures. Working *with* foreign competitors is one way of reducing these uncertainties.

In conclusion, European governments would seem to be justified in following a two-track policy. They can continue to develop intra-European policies designed to improve the underlying competitive-ness of the European economy and companies – even though it will steadily become harder to exclude Japanese-owned subsidiaries from participating. At the same time, they should carefully encourage Japanese inward investment as a way of maintaining competitive pressure on European companies. They should also be broadly positive towards more narrowly collaborative ventures between European and Japanese companies in those cases when European companies favour this. Japan has much to offer western economies, so collaboration – whether according to Japan's wider definition or Europe's narrower one – makes sense.

NOTES

1. Very confusingly, this British automobile company has changed its name twice in recent years. Once known as 'British Leyland', it has successively become 'BL' and, in 1986, 'The Rover Group'. The Honda collaboration has been with the high-volume car division of this company, which is known as the 'Austin-Rover Group'.
2. A term popularized in Kenichi Ohmae's *Triad Power: The Coming Shape of Global Competition* (London: Collier Macmillan, 1985).
3. Keijiro Murata, 'Stronger Japan-EC relations and the deepening of industrial cooperation', speech to the Fourth Japan-EC Symposium, 30 September/1 October 1985.
4. My thanks to Helen Wallace and Brian Bridges for this analysis. I have decided against trying to coin a new term to cover the wider Japanese use of the words 'industrial collaboration', but I have been careful to make it clear when issues related to 100% direct investment are being discussed.
5. Study Group on Japanese Direct Foreign Investment (supported by MITI), *Japanese direct foreign investment: a new multidimensional approach. Contributing to the vitalization of the world economy* (Summary), 16 August 1985, pp. 6–7.
6. Hernan Molina, 'The US revalues its electronics patents', *New Scientist*, 1 May 1986, p. 40.
7. Geoffrey Charlish, 'Why rivals club together', *The Financial Times*, 23 January 1986.
8. For instance, Japan's whisky industry came about as the result of one man's study trip in 1918–20 to Glasgow University and the then thriving whisky centre of Campbeltown. See Bob Johnstone, 'Japan thinks whisky', *New Scientist*, 19 December 1985, p. 19.
9. John Stopford and Louis Turner, *Britain and the Multinationals* (Chichester: Wiley, 1985); interview with Shinichi Saitoh, former Chairman of Sumitomo Rubber, in *DATAR News Review*, no. 37 (winter 1985/6), p. 9.

10. See Dan Fenno Henderson, *Foreign Enterprise in Japan* (Chapel Hill: University of North Carolina Press, 1974), pp. 13–14, for further examples.
11. Simon Caulkin, 'Fujitsu sights its futures', *Management Today*, December 1985, p. 65.
12. *Liberal Star* (Tokyo), 10 February 1985, pp. 10–11.
13. Yoshi Tsurumi, *The Japanese are Coming* (Cambridge, MA: Ballinger, 1976), pp. 21–3.
14. Firms like Ford and General Motors had established Japanese subsidiaries in the 1920s, which they lost control of in the run-up to World War II.
15. K. Kojima, *Direct Foreign Investment* (London: Croom Helm, 1978); T. Ozawa, *Multinationalism, Japanese Style* (Princeton, NJ: Princeton University Press, 1979).
16. 'Japanese investment in the US: creating jobs and narrowing the trade deficit', *Backgrounder* (Asian Studies Centre, Heritage Foundation), 16 April 1986, pp. 1–3.
17. Naohiro Amaya, 'Toward the further development of Japan-EC industrial cooperation, with special reference to Japan-UK relations', paper to the United Kingdom-Japan 2000 Group (London and Tokyo), January 1986.
18. Ozawa, *Multinationalism*, pp. 227, 231.
19. 'Philips to build VHS video-recorder factory in Japan', *The Financial Times*, 17 September 1985.
20. *Japan Economic Journal*, 27 February 1979, p. 15.
21. *Japan Economic Journal*, 23 December 1980, p. 11.
22. Japanese readers should note that some of the strongest comments from European readers of the drafts of this paper centred on the Japanese motives described here. More than one reader considered that they were imperialist and reminiscent of the days when the British and other imperialists believed that they had a mission to bring civilization to less developed parts of the world. This strong response from readers who have a relatively international outlook should alert Japanese policy-makers to some sensitivities among the western powers that they have been 'overhauling'.
23. For a particularly detailed analysis of the pressures affecting Japanese policy-makers, see Kazuo Nukazawa, 'The making of foreign economic policy', in Loukas Tsoukalis and Maureen White (eds), *Japan and Western Europe* (London: Pinter, 1982), pp. 56–79.
24. Nukazawa, 'The making of foreign economic policy', p. 66.
25. For a reference to this revitalization theme in 1982, see Nukazawa, 'The making of foreign economic policy', p. 66.
26. John H. Dunning, *Japanese Participation in British Industry* (London: Croom Helm, 1986), p. 6.
27. See John Stopford and Louis Turner, *Britain and the Multinationals*, pp. 198, 256, 262.
28. 'France leads Europe in attracting Japanese', *The Financial Times*, 12 June 1986.

29. *Q & A: Trading with Japan* (Tokyo: Keizai Koho Centre, 1985), p. 9.
30. This is a fairly rare example of a Japanese company acquiring a non-Japanese one. See *Management-Transfer*, vol. 1, no. 1, pp. 4–7, for some impressions on how Sony-Wega is managed.
31. The Betriebsverfassungsgesetz and Mitbestimmungsgesetz are the two laws which regulate worker participation in German industry.
32. See Hans-Peter Merz, 'Japanese subsidiaries in the Federal Republic of Germany: relating to the Betriebsrat', *Management-Transfer*, vol. 1, no. 1, p. 10, for an account which stresses the problems Japanese managements face in coming to terms with these obligations.
33. *Japan Economic Journal*, 28 July 1981, p. 19.
34. *The Economist*, 24 August 1985, p. 75.
35. *Japan Economic Journal*, 14 July 1981, p. 3.
36. Alan Cawson, Geoffrey Shepherd and Douglas Webber, 'Government-industry relations in the European consumer electronics industry: contrasting responses to competitive pressures in Britain, France and West Germany', paper presented to the Annual Conference of the Political Studies Association, University of Nottingham, April 1986, p. 4.
37. PAL technology was used by all European countries with the exception of France. See 'Setting a control on Japanese imports', *New Scientist*, 31 October 1985, p. 27, for a brief evaluation of how EMI's licensing manager, Mr Fred Evans, handled these negotiations through the 1960s and 1970s.
38. Ian Aitken, 'Tokyo commentary', *The Guardian*, 3 March 1986, p. 19.
39. This was very much an extension of the Import Promotion Mission, which was sponsored by the two governments in early 1979. *Japan Economic Journal*, 16 January 1979.
40. *Japan Economic Journal*, 24 June 1980, pp. 1–2.
41. Alan Cawson, Peter Holmes and Anne Stevens, 'The interaction between firms and the state in France: the telecommunications and consumer electronics sectors', paper presented to a conference on Government-Industry Relations in the Major OECD Countries, sponsored by the Economic and Social Research Council, Cambridge, 10–13 December 1985.
42. David Marsh, 'Sumitomo Rubber: breaking the mould of old practices', *The Financial Times*, 7 March 1986.
43. *Japan Economic Journal*, 29 July 1980, p. 3.
44. This section is largely based on Michael Hodges's work.
45. 'Japanese investment', *Backgrounder*, p. 3.
46. *New York Times*, 26 February 1985. The relatively fragmented nature of the US approach to Japanese investors does not seem to have discouraged them as much as the lack of central direction seems to have done in West Germany.
47. Joan Walsh, 'The Fremont experiment', *Management-Transfer*, vol. 1, no. 1, pp. 14–19.
48. *Business Week*, 14 July 1986, pp. 51–2.

49. See Gene Gregory, 'Asia's electronics revolution', *Euro-Asia Business Review*, vol. 1, no. 1, pp. 42–54, for an authoritative analysis of the emergence after 1945 of the industry in East Asia.
50. 'The hollow corporation', *Business Week*, 3 March 1986, p. 53.
51. 'Philips chief says electronics in US in danger', *International Herald Tribune*, 29 March 1986, p. 7.
52. See Cawson, Shepherd and Webber, 'Government-industry', pp. 5–6, for a detailed analysis of British policy during this period. NEDO was set up in the 1960s to bring industrialists, civil servants and trade unionists together to discuss British economic and industrial strategies. What were known in the 1970s as Sector Working Parties are committees, drawn from the three sides of the debate, which concentrate on the problems and prospects of specific industrial sectors.
53. For an earlier treatment of these issues, see Louis Turner, 'Consumer electronics: the colour television case', in Louis Turner and Neil McMullen (eds), *The Newly Industrializing Countries: Trade and Adjustment* (London: Allen and Unwin for the RIIA, 1982); Cawson, Shepherd and Webber, 'Government-industry', pp. 3–8; and Robert Ballance and Stuart Sinclair, *Collapse and Survival: Industry Strategies in a Changing World* (London: Allen and Unwin, 1983), pp. 130–42.
54. Geoffrey Shepherd, 'The Japanese challenge to Western Europe's new crisis industries', *World Economy*, December 1981, pp. 375–90.
55. Mr Mita is quoted in 'Japan's growing international investment', the 24th annual advertising supplement in *Fortune*, 19 August 1985. See also John Dunning, *Japanese Participation*, pp. 168–70; and Philip Bassett, *Strike Free: New Industrial Relations in Britain* (London: Macmillan, 1986), pp. 122–38.
56. Bassett, *Strike Free*.
57. *The Financial Times*, 25 March 1986, p. 24.
58. Joan Pearce and John Sutton, with Roy Batchelor, *Protection and Industrial Policy in Europe* (London: Routledge & Kegan Paul for the RIIA, 1986), pp. 156–7. Cawson, Holmes and Stevens, 'The interaction', pp. 26–30.
59. Adrian Hamilton, 'The outposts of an exports empire', *The Observer*, 16 June 1985.
60. A system whereby text is broadcast over the air to slightly modified television sets in the United Kingdom; Ceefax and Oracle are two examples.
61. Jurek Martin, 'Japanese urged to scrap export targeting', *The Financial Times*, 26 March 1986 (interview with Dr Wisse Dekker).
62. This section relies heavily on the work of Konomi Tomisawa and Reinhard Hild.
63. Alan Friedman, 'Alfa Romeo takes the "Tramontana cure"', *The Financial Times*, 17 March 1986.
64. The Isuzu and Suzuki ties are quite complex. When Suzuki accepted GM's equity participation of 5.3% in 1981, it entered into an interlocking equity arrangement with Isuzu (in which GM had a 32.2%

stake). Suzuki took a 1.32% stake in Isuzu, and Isuzu took a 3.5% stake in Suzuki.

65. This section is based on the work of Konomi Tomisawa and Ralph-Dieter Mayer.
66. Simon Caulkin, 'Fujitsu sights its futures', p. 66.
67. Laura Raun and Peter Bruce, 'Europe's risky dash to catch up in microchips', *The Financial Times*, 14 March 1986.
68. Raun and Bruce, 'Europe's risky dash'.
69. The fact that the French withdrew is symptomatic of the dilemmas faced by European policy-makers. In a number of cases, European companies have preferred to enter into collaborations with non-European companies rather than give an advantage to a European competitor.
70. Caulkin, 'Fujitsu sights its futures', p. 66.
71. Complementary Metal-Oxide Semiconductors.
72. Japan's leading electronics company, NEC, preaches 'C&C' as its gospel for future success. See *The Economist*, 12 April 1986, pp. 77–80, for an analysis of NEC's overall strategies.
73. Bob Johnstone, 'Japan unveils its fifth-generation', *New Scientist*, 8 November 1984, pp. 10–11.
74. A semi-official explanation of Japan's position is that, 'The Japanese government will grant licences to any companies for any industrial property rights arising in a non-discriminatory manner regardless of their nationalities.' Amaya, 'Toward the further development of Japan-EC industrial cooperation'.
75. Ibid.
76. This section is based on work done by Michael Hodges and Yoshi-hisa Miyanaga.
77. Rosalie L. Tung, *Business Negotiations with the Japanese* (Lexington, MA: Lexington Books, 1984), pp. 115–17.
78. Ian Rodger, 'All systems go as Japan soars into space', *The Financial Times*, 14 August 1986; 'Some rockets still work', *The Economist*, 16 August 1986, p. 85.
79. Bruce Kogut and Harbir Singh, 'Entering the United States by acquisition or joint venture: country patterns and cultural characteristics', paper presented to the Conference of the Association of International Business, Strathclyde University, December 1986.
80. Interim report by the Industrial Structure Council, MITI, 'An outlook for Japan's industrial society towards the 21st century' (Tokyo: Ministry of International Trade and Industry, February 1986), p. 8.
81. Dunning, *Japanese Participation*; Turner and Stopford, *Britain and the Multinationals*; Bassett, *Strike Free*; Malcolm Trevor, *Japan's Reluctant Multinationals* (London: Frances Pinter, 1983).
82. Dunning, *Japanese Participation*, pp. 144–7, gives some of the conflicting responses of British competitors to Japanese investors in the United Kingdom.
83. *Business Week*, 14 July 1986, p. 50.

84. Dunning, *Japanese Participation*, p. 103.
85. Amaya, 'Toward the further development of Japan-EC industrial cooperation'.
86. *Business Week*, 14 July 1986, p. 55; *The Financial Times*, 1 July 1986, p. 19.
87. Dunning, *Japanese Participation*, p. 155.
88. Japanese readers may find this accusation distasteful, but it is a common charge in the West. It is not supported by this study, but it has to be acknowledged.
89. This sentence was worded with some care. The analysis of IBM's relationship with its Japanese competitors triggered some of the more sensitive negotiations between the Japanese and non-Japanese researchers on this project.
90. Bob Johnstone, 'Japanese industry files a countersuit', *New Scientist*, 1 May 1986, p. 42.
91. The forthcoming Chatham House Paper *European Technological Collaboration*, by Margaret Sharp and Claire Shearman, describes the background to these European initiatives, and to a large extent complements the analysis in this paper.
92. Robert Reich and Eric Mankin, 'Joint ventures with Japan give away our future', *Harvard Business Review*, March/April 1986, pp. 78–86.
93. Mark Snowden, 'Austin-Rover: the links with Honda', address to the Society of Strategic and Long Range Planning, London, 22 November 1985.
94. Japan Trade Offices.
95. Amaya, 'Toward the further development of Japan-EC industrial cooperation', section III; 'Japanese Ministry of International Trade and Industry to allow foreign firms to participate in joint planning meetings', *Asahi News Service*, October 1984.
96. Here is a typical quote, from a former chairman of the European Business Council in Japan: 'When we deal with Japan, we think we are dealing with a country like ours. Japan is more like a Third World country suddenly gone rich. They have got to get used to the idea. It's just a matter of time.' *Fortune*, 21 July 1986, p. 76.

Related forthcoming title

European Technological Collaboration
Margaret Sharp and Claire Shearman
(Chatham House Paper No. 36)

West European industries need to compete in tough international markets if they are to hold their own against American and Japanese firms. This competition is especially rigorous in high-technology sectors, and one response among European industries and their governments has been to promote greater collaboration both in research and development and in new manufacturing and marketing initiatives. This paper begins by examining the relative position of West European industry in high-technology sectors, and the moves towards collaboration both by industrialists and by governments and the European Community itself (including such initiatives as Esprit and Eureka). It concludes with an analysis of the case for and against collaboration at a European level, asking how far it is actually promoting greater competitiveness, and how far governments, and the UK government in particular, should be actively promoting European, as distinct from multinational, collaboration. This subject is clearly of prime importance not only to industrialists themselves, but also to the academics and policy-makers working on industrial policy.

Margaret Sharp is a Senior Research Fellow at the Science Policy Research Unit, University of Sussex. She co-authored an earlier Chatham House Paper (No. 21) with Michael Brech on *Inward Investment: Policy Options for the United Kingdom* (1984). Claire Shearman is currently a Research Associate at the University of Lancaster, having moved there from the Department of Science and Technology Policy at Manchester University.

ROUTLEDGE & KEGAN PAUL